EUROPE: GOVERNMENT and MONEY

Running EMU: the challenges of policy co-ordination

edited by
Iain Begg

THE FEDERAL TRUST
for education & research

This book is published by the Federal Trust, whose aim is to enlighten public debate on federal issues of national, continental and global governance. It does this in the light of its statutes which state that it shall promote 'studies in the principles of international relations, international justice and supranational government.'

The Federal Trust conducts enquiries, promotes seminars and conferences and publishes reports and teaching materials. It is the UK member of the Trans-European Policy Studies Association (TEPSA), a grouping of fifteen think-tanks from member states of the European Union.

Up-to-date information about the Federal Trust can be found on the internet at www.fedtrust.co.uk

© Federal Trust for Education and Research 2002

ISBN 1 903403 35 9

NOTE: All contributors to this volume are writing in a personal capacity. Views expressed are those of the authors and do not represent the position of their institution.

The Federal Trust is a Registered Charity No. 272241

Dean Bradley House, 52 Horseferry Road,

London SW1P 2AF

Company Limited by Guarantee No.1269848

Marketing and Distribution by Kogan Page Ltd

Printed by J W Arrowsmith Ltd

Contents

Notes on Contributors

Christopher Allsopp is Fellow in Economics at New College, Oxford and a Member of the Monetary Policy Committee of the Bank of England.

Ray Barrell is a Senior Research Fellow at the National Institute of Economic and Social Research in London, where he leads the World Economy team.

Iain Begg is a Fellow at the European Institute at the London School of Economics and the co-editor of the *Journal of Common Market Studies*.

Robert Boyer is Director of Research at the CNRS, economist at CEPREMAP in Paris and a member of the French *Conseil d'Analyse Economique*.

Nicos Christodoulakis is Minister of Economy and Finance of Greece and became President of the Eurogroup in July 2002.

Diane Coyle is the Director of Enlightenment Economics, a consultancy specialising in global and technological issues, and was previously the Economics Editor of *The Independent*.

Klaus Gretschmann is Director General in the *General Secretariat of the Council* and served as Chief Economist and Personal Representative for G8 Summits to German Chancellor Gerhard Schröder.

Christopher Huhne is a Liberal Democrat Member of the European Parliament for South East England and a Member of its Economic and Monetary Affairs Committee.

Otmar Issing is a Member of the Executive Board of the ECB and the Bank's Chief Economist, and served from 1990 until 1998 as a Member of the Board of the Deutsche Bundesbank.

Jacques Le Cacheux is Professor of Economics at the Université de Pau et des Pays de l'Adour and Director of the Economic Research Department at the OFCE in Paris.

Pier Carlo Padoan is Professor of Economics at the University of Rome and Executive Director of the International Monetary Fund, and was a special adviser on economic policy to the Italian Prime Minister.

Martin Weale CBE, is Director of the National Institute of Economic and Social Research in London and a member of the UK's Statistics Commission.

Sir Nigel Wicks chairs the Committee on Standards in Public Life and the board of CRESTCo Ltd. He was Second Permanent Secretary at HM Treasury and Director of International Finance, and President of the EU Monetary Committee, 1993-98.

Acknowledgements

This book arose from a discussion of future projects at a meeting of the Council of the Federal Trust in September 2001. A consensus rapidly formed that the Trust ought to publish a study explaining and analysing the emerging machinery for the conduct of economic policy in the euro area. By serendipity, a research project I was directing on roughly this theme was nearing its conclusion, and I was rapidly volunteered for a job which has been a highly enjoyable one.

Many people have facilitated the production of this book. The authors of the chapters are, without exception, extraordinarily busy and I am especially grateful to all of them for carving out time to write such stimulating papers. My thanks, too, to Nicos Christodoulakis who, despite his onerous responsibilities agreed immediately to my request that he write the Foreword. The funding received from the UK's Economic and Social Research Council for research project L213252034 provided invaluable resources, and my colleagues on the project, Brian Ardy, Dermot Hodson, Imelda Maher and Sarah Plant have all helped to bring this book to fruition. I have benefited throughout from the support of the Council of the Federal Trust, its Director and staff. In particular, I am delighted to sing the praises of Dusan Jakovljevic who did all the hard work needed to turn disparate chapters, formats and styles into a coherent text.

Iain Begg
August 2002

Foreword

It is generally recognised that the Economic and Monetary union is a bold and historic shift in the economic governance of Europe. It is vitally important for our future prosperity that it succeeds. The transition to the euro has been surprisingly smooth and the ease with which the citizens of the euro area countries have adapted to the single currency has been remarkable. Nevertheless, it is incumbent upon all of us involved in policy-making to consolidate these achievements. As Minister of Economy and Finance of a small euro area country but also as the chairman of the Eurogroup, I am well aware of the need to continue to develop the economic policy machinery, so that EMU is able to fulfil its potential for growth and stability.

Although the Stability and Growth Pact and the Broad Economic Policy Guidelines will remain at the heart of policy-making, running EMU will call for imaginative new thinking on how to improve economic policy making and to integrate policy in other domains, while respecting the imperatives of subsidiarity. I therefore welcome the valuable contributions in this book to the debate on how policy-making should evolve. The eleven essays examine important questions for the future conduct of policy under EMU and offer a wide-ranging analysis of the issues, focusing particularly on the difficult question of policy co-ordination. We shall be soon discussing what the scope of co-ordination should be, and how we can improve policy making, in the EMU. These are all big questions for the coming years.

The authors, who include many friends and colleagues from my own days as an economics professor, present contrasting and provocative views on economic policy. As is customary among economists, the authors do not agree on either the need for more extensive policy co-ordination or the forms that it might take. But in developing the arguments, they show the complexity of the issues, identify options for change and remind us of the work still to be done to assure the success of EMU. A virtue of the book is that it not only contains incisive analyses of the challenges of securing an appropriate mix of monetary and fiscal policy, but also confronts supply-side matters and the international representation of the euro area.

I am sure that many of the topics covered in the book will surface in the discussions of the Eurogroup and Ecofin over the next year, and that my fellow finance ministers and I will soon be trying to resolve many of the issues raised in this book.

Nicos Christodoulakis
Minister of Economy and Finance of Greece
and President of the Eurogroup

July 2002

Running Economic and Monetary Union: the challenges of policy co-ordination

Iain Begg[*]

Introduction

Economic and monetary union in the EU (EMU) is still in its infancy and it will be some time before it reaches maturity as an economic policy system. Nevertheless, and belying many of the more apocalyptic predictions about what could and would go wrong, the early years of the euro have been marked by a successful transition to what is, after all, a profoundly different policy regime. Monetary policy has moved seamlessly from the member states of the EU to the European Central Bank (ECB) and, despite some turbulence and growing pressures for reforms, fiscal policy has remained broadly consistent with the rules, procedures and directions embodied in the Stability and Growth Pact (SGP) and the Broad Economic Policy Guidelines (BEPGs).

Bodies designed to promote the effective conduct of policy, such as the Economic and Financial Committee (EFC) and the Economic Policy Committee (EPC), both of which discuss major economic policy issues and 'prepare' decisions for the Ecofin Council, are reported to function effectively. Although the absence of three member states (Denmark, Sweden and the UK) from the single currency has complicated matters institutionally, the

* I am greatful to the ESRC for financial support (under project L213252034) as part of the *One Europe or Several?* research programme.

informal Eurogroup, composed of representatives of the participating countries, has (according to recent research[1]) worked well as a forum for, above all, discussing the political choices in economic policy-making.

Machinery has, in parallel, been put in place to ensure that the supply side of the EU economy is not neglected. The European Employment Strategy (EES), especially what is known as the Luxembourg Process, has now been through four complete annual cycles and is proving to be effective as a means of pushing member states to rethink how they modernise their labour markets, although it is, perhaps, too soon to judge whether it has had a clear-cut effect on outcomes. Building on the agreement reached at the Cardiff European Council in 1998, the special Lisbon European Council held in March 2000 set out an ambitious agenda for restoring the impetus towards completion of the internal market, boosting the EU employment rate and making the EU 'the most competitive and dynamic knowledge-based economy in the world' by 2010 (European Council, 2000: paragraph 5). It also initiated annual reviews each spring, and these have now taken place at the Stockholm (2001) and Barcelona (2002) European Councils.

Although there was disappointment in some quarters at the sluggish pace of reforms – especially what was finally agreed at the Barcelona meeting – and the reluctance of some member states to conform, a preliminary verdict on how EMU, as a policy system, is being run might nevertheless be 'so far, so good'.

To co-ordinate or not?

Yet for many, there is still a profound concern about whether the current institutional architecture is appropriate for the policy challenges the EU faces. Critics maintain that the ECB is too powerful and unaccountable, that the arrangements for fiscal policy are incoherent and will not withstand a serious downturn or increasingly divergent national trends, and that (notwithstanding the recovery from the US-led recession in 2001) the apparent success of the early years of the euro is illusory. In particular the diffuse and tentative nature of the mechanisms for policy co-ordination is often cited as a fundamental weakness.

Given that the Treaty explicitly obliges the member states to co-ordinate their policies (Article 4, which establishes principles, and Article 99, which details how), it might be thought that all that is required is agreement on procedures. Indeed, there is already a reasonably developed range of mechanisms for co-ordinating different forms of policy – see Commission (2002) for a presentation of the various channels through which policy is currently co-ordinated – while the 'invention' at the 2000 Lisbon European Council of the open method of co-ordination (OMC) provides for a novel approach. It is clear, however, that there are strongly held and divergent views on what should (and should not) be co-ordinated and thus on the need for further development.

The first aim of this book is to assess whether the policy machinery currently in place is sufficient for running EMU effectively, and if not, whether more extensive policy co-ordination might enhance the quality of economic governance of the euro area. At one level, the answer is intuitively positive: to the extent that co-ordination means that the various actors agree what needs to be done and act accordingly, it must be 'a good thing'. By the same token, if the huskies all pull in different directions, the sled will rapidly embed itself in a snowdrift. Is there, therefore, a case for looking beyond the current mechanisms to ask whether institutional reforms are needed to enhance the conduct of policy? A second aim of this book is to look afresh at what is meant by the term co-ordination and to explore how it is functioning at present in the EU.

The book brings together a distinguished group of contributors, from both policy-making and academic backgrounds, who nevertheless exhibit the customary propensity to discordance of economists. Equally, the contributions show that there are awkward questions to be confronted in consolidating EMU and in developing the policy framework. The next two sections of this introductory essay present an outline of the book and briefly describe the current arrangements for policy co-ordination in running EMU. Various dimensions of co-ordination are then explored in greater depth to try to establish what is broadly agreed and what is contested. A concluding section reviews the unfinished business in relation to economic management of EMU and speculates on how the policy system behind the euro may be expected to evolve.

Outline of the book

The first two essays in the book concentrate on the overall structure of the emerging policy system. Nigel Wicks sets the scene by explaining how economic management at the EU level differs fundamentally from the standard textbook analyses of 'policy mix' or economic management at the level of the nation-state. He points out that insofar as the Treaty provides for co-ordination, it is in relation to the 'E' in EMU, that is between the respective government ministries responsible for economic policy (above all, finance ministries), but *not* between the economic authorities and the ECB. Acknowledging the political sensitivities of co-ordination, especially for certain member states, he proposes a limited menu of co-ordination tasks. Robert Boyer then broadens the debate by drawing attention to potential problems that arise from the character of the policy machinery. He cautions against a monolithic view of the world in which there is a sole agreed 'true model', arguing instead that there are many facets of policy that require not only greater co-ordination, but in which competing views of how the economy works can be entertained. He concludes that a counterpart to the powerful monetary authority – the ECB – is needed to achieve better-balanced policy and makes the case for the establishment of a *gouvernement économique*.

Otmar Issing persuasively makes the case that if each policy actor sticks strictly to its mandate, the optimal outcome will be achieved, because confusion about roles and accountability will, thereby, be minimised. Drawing on his unparalleled experience as a policy-maker, he asserts that the advocates of more extensive macroeconomic co-ordination do not take sufficient account of the political economy of policy-making. He also emphasises the importance of structural policies in dealing with adjustment problems. Ray Barrell and Martin Weale argue, however, that it is important to pay attention to the macroeconomic policy mix and that some overall co-ordinating mechanism is, consequently, desirable. They recall that fiscal policy is bound to affect inflation rates as well as other macroeconomic variables and suggest that the interdependencies between policy instruments have been insufficiently taken into account.

Chris Allsopp also points to concerns about the manner in which fiscal policies set at national level dovetail with monetary policy. He goes on to identify specific difficulties about EMU as a policy system that require attention, notably the inter-actions between the labour market and macroeconomic management, and the ramifications of current account imbalances. He explains that under EMU, shifts in relative competitiveness will have to play a greater role in securing economic adjustment and stresses the need for supply-side policies to be determined in parallel with the demand side, thereby widening the scope of policy co-ordination. Pier Carlo Padoan also explores policy questions that bridge the demand and supply sides of policy-making, focusing especially on employment policies covered by the Luxembourg Process. He notes that two frequent criticisms of monetary union are that the euro area is not an optimal currency area and that it suffers from an institutional imbalance in that separate national policy-makers cannot match the coherence of a single monetary authority. He maintains, however, that the reconfiguration of macroeconomic policy consequent upon EMU will progressively stimulate changes in microeconomic policy that will, *ex-post*, make the euro area more optimal as a currency area, and is, consequently reasonably sanguine about the outlook as a gradual piecing together of co-ordination mechanisms occurs.

Other aspects of the political of economy of EMU are explored in the essays by Chris Huhne and Klaus Gretschmann. The former maintains that the current structure for policy-making is about right, at least for the time being, but that there is considerable room for improvement in presentation and in fostering broader debate on policy. He argues that economic governance might, however, be improved by revisiting some of the current rules and by co-ordinating demand and supply-side policies more explicitly. Policy would also be greatly enhanced by being more transparent and by being subject to more intensive scrutiny, especially by the European Parliament. Gretschmann, while also hesitant about major changes, carefully explains many of the dilemmas of greater co-ordination and the lack of agreement on so many key issues. He draws attention to certain areas where confusion remains, notably in the external representation of the euro in fora such as the G8 or the international financial institutions[2], and puts forward suggestions for overcoming these inadequacies.

Two essays then look in greater detail at specific supply side issues, emphasising the point made in earlier chapters that co-ordination has to extend well beyond conventional macroeconomic policy. Diane Coyle looks at how policies to promote productivity and the new economy – key elements of the 'Lisbon' agenda to modernise the EU economy – fit together. She expresses concerns about the slow pace with which the EU has embraced structural reforms and calls for bolder approaches, stressing that there is no inevitability about success. Jacques Le Cacheux analyses the implications for policy co-ordination of long-run demographic change and the resulting pressures on pensions. He explains how these trends call for fresh thinking about how savings and investment balances are distributed, not only among the euro area countries, but also between the EU and the rest of the world. Although the December 2001 Laeken European Council agreed to apply the OMC for pensions, it remains an open question whether this goes far enough.

Current arrangements in the euro area

In an economy as large and complex as that of the EU, it might be thought of as a statement of the obvious to say that the machinery for economic policy decision-making has to be centralised to some degree. The EU is far less united politically than typical federal countries, yet has manifestly evolved to be much more than a free-trade area. Policy, consequently, has to navigate carefully between the independent preferences and jealously guarded powers of often prickly member states and the common imperatives of coherent and appropriate policy.

Looking at EMU today, the position is that there is a rule-based system for co-ordination of fiscal policy, embodied in the SGP (see Box 1 opposite), looser co-ordination of employment policy through the EES and a form of soft overall co-ordination through the BEPGs. In addition, pensions (see the chapter by Le Cacheux), other facets of the supply side (discussed in the chapter by Coyle) and social inclusion are now subject to 'processes' or variants of the OMC that try to assure a degree of commonality in policy approaches. The different forms of co-ordination are very varied in character and face differing problems. Collectively, as the chapters in this volume by Allsopp, by Boyer and by Barrell and Weale show, the policy system as a whole is open to the criticism that it is unsatisfactory and needs to be bolstered by some form of *gouvernement économique*.

Box 1

THE STABILITY AND GROWTH PACT: CENTREPIECE OF POLICY CO-ORDINATION UNDER EMU?

The principal policy device for co-ordinating fiscal policy under EMU is the Stability and Growth Pact (SGP). In principle, the Pact is a component of the wider co-ordination machinery provided for in Article 99 of the *Treaty* and, as such, constitutes one 'pillar' for the achievement of the *Broad Economic Policy Guidelines* (BEPGs). The latter, however, only have the status of recommendations, whereas the SGP imposes obligations on member states.

The purpose of the SGP is to maintain the fiscal disciplines that the 'Maastricht' convergence criteria imposed on countries that wanted to be part of the single currency.

Its **legal base** is an agreement reached at the 1996 Dublin European Council, formally adopted as a resolution six months later at Amsterdam, and given force in two Council regulations agreed in 1997 (1466/97 and 1467/97). The first regulation covers surveillance and co-ordination of economic polices, while the second stipulates what constitutes an excessive deficit and how the rules are to be enforced.

Targets are central to the Pact which constrains member states by restricting the permissible size of the budget deficit to **3 per cent of GDP** in the short-term and prescribing a medium-term target of **'close to balance or in surplus'**. In exceptional circumstances, defined as a fall in GDP of at least 2 per cent, a member state is allowed to breach the 3 per cent limit.

Surveillance of member states entails the regular production and updating of *Convergence Programmes* for those countries not yet participating fully in stage 3 of EMU and *Stability Programmes* for euro area countries. In practice, they cover very similar ground in setting out short- and medium-term plans that show how fiscal disciplines will be respected. These are monitored by the Commission and considered periodically by Ecofin.

Sanctions can be imposed on member states that breach the 3 per cent rule, but only after a protracted process involving warnings and peer pressures. In theory a country that fails to rein in an excessive deficit sufficiently promptly could be subjected to financial penalties in the form, initially, of a non-interest bearing deposit, but with the further threat that this will be converted into a fine. Most informed commentators believe that the financial penalties are unlikely ever to be imposed, and the expectation is that peer pressures will be sufficient to avert problems.

For a succinct presentation of the institutional framework for policy co-ordination, see European Commission (2002).

Within the SGP, co-ordination encompasses sanctions as well as prescriptions, although as the debate in the run up to the Seville European Council in June 2002 showed, there is (deliberate?) ambiguity about how rapidly countries should conform to the 'close to balance or in surplus' target and what should be done if they are recalcitrant. Nevertheless, the SGP tends to be perceived as having teeth, even if the jaw muscles do not seem to allow for much of a bite, and this is a conception with which economists raised in the 'rules' rather than 'discretion' tradition are relatively comfortable. These rules should, in principle, ensure that national fiscal stances are sufficiently convergent to avoid problems. A further metaphor that has been used to capture this[3] is that of a rowing eight where, if the rowers do not co-ordinate their strokes, the boat will make no progress and might even capsize.

The perpetual contest between the supranational institutions and inter-governmentalism adds a further twist. A new approach that favours the latter – the open method of co-ordination – has found favour in recent years, at a time when calls for new pan-European policy bodies face growing opposition. The OMC, arguably, is an approach that tries to reconcile the desire for national autonomy with the imperative of a common policy orientation and is, consequently, suited to the current political economy of the EU. Its principal advantages are that it provides the means to move towards common solutions to common problems without demanding the sort of harmonisation that would be anathema to many governments, and that it can be implemented by governments without recourse to major and potentially contested legislative change. Moreover, by allowing countries to shape national programmes within common guidelines, OMC allows governments to weight their policy packages appropriately. In the rowing metaphor, the rowers will be pulling in harmony, but one will have an oar, another might be using a paddle, while a third has a shovel.

Opponents of OMC are in two camps: those who believe that resort to the method is a device to avoid the hard decisions about what is needed to run EMU effectively; and those who see it as a Trojan horse for an inevitable (but almost certainly misguided) transfer of economic policy competence to the demon 'Brussels'. There is, in addition, a tension at the heart of OMC: the more strictly any targets are monitored, the less the discretion available to a Member State in shaping programmes. At the same time, if there is no sanction for failing to adopt suitable measures (or, as was the case for the EMU convergence criteria, a reward), let alone meeting targets, the attempt to co-ordinate could prove to be empty.

Although the European Employment Strategy – the flag-bearer for OMC – appears to be working tolerably well in its own terms, what is less clear is how it fits into the overall conduct of policy under EMU. There are three distinct issues here: first, the success of the EES in stimulating employment in the EU; second, whether the content of the strategy assists macroeconomic adjustment; and third, whether it is adequately co-ordinated with demand-side policies and with other supply-side measures. A reasonably positive view can be taken of the first, since the evidence of employment trends suggests that there has been some improvement in the underlying rate of job creation, although the recovery from the downturn of 2001 will be the real test.

Turning to its broader role in the policy system, the EES has, arguably, contributed to a general rethinking of how labour market adjustment can be achieved, although it is open to the criticism that too many of the guidelines are tangential to an adjustment strategy. Some critics, such as Visser (2002) argue that there has also been an undue concentration on what he identifies as the OECD (as in the 1994 'Jobs Study') viewpoint in which liberalisation and deregulation of labour markets is crucial. Hence it is much less clear how it contributes to adjustment or whether it is sufficiently integrated with fiscal and monetary policy. This latter concern is even more acute for the other supply-side policies discussed in subsequent chapters.

Policy co-ordination: an elusive concept?

At its simplest, co-ordination can be portrayed as procedures to ensure that choices made in one policy domain do not have unwanted repercussions in another. Co-ordination can function at multiple levels and in diverse ways. It can be tacit or explicit; based on strongly prescriptive rules or informality; statutory or voluntary. It could mean a *de facto* process of negotiation in which a concession here on monetary policy brings forth an accommodation there on fiscal policy or sweet reason in the labour market. In this sense, co-ordination would imply the joint setting of the main instruments so that explicit optimisation of the policy mix – however defined – is the aim: this might be called *vertical* co-ordination.

Or, as Otmar Issing explains in his essay in this volume, the best outcomes might be achieved by policy-makers sticking meticulously to their mandates. The aphorism used by Alesina et al. (2001) is *keep your houses in order*: do so and all will be well. Clarity of objectives and accountability may thus be the way to assure efficient policy-making, with co-ordination confined to the pursuit of common (or mutually consistent) positions within a policy area, such as fiscal policy (we might label this *horizontal*).

In short, a seemingly obvious concept is open to contrasting and often contradictory interpretations. The difficulties are exemplified by the dilemmas surrounding fiscal policy which, in any currency union, will inevitably have to be subject to some agreements among the members of the union to prevent spillovers from one country to another. But the collective fiscal stance also matters, because it will bear on the interplay between fiscal and monetary policy.

In many federal countries, lower tiers of government are often subject to fiscal disciplines imposed by constitutional rules that restrict or prohibit the right to run a fiscal deficit, such as the balanced budget rule that most US states have chosen to adopt. Any discretionary fiscal policy is then confined to what the federal tier of government does. Clearly, with a tiny central budget capped at 1.27 per cent of GDP, the EU level cannot fulfil this function, so that stabilisation through fiscal policy is necessarily the task of member states.

A more ambitious form of co-ordination would imply joint decision-making in which choices in different domains of policy are made simultaneously in order to optimise outcomes across a range of target variables. In the traditional theory of economic policy going back to Jan Tinbergen and James Meade (see the chapter by Barrell and Weale), this led to the notion of the policy mix and the requirement of at least as many policy instruments as targets if the system of simultaneous equations used in mathematical models to describe this approach is capable of solution. As the chapter by Nigel Wicks explains, the policy mix notion was essentially about demand management in a Keynesian world with a single monetary authority facing an equivalent fiscal policy actor. Many contemporary analyses try to recapture this inter-action in the more complex world of EMU using game theory (for example, Buti et al, 2001). However, a wider scope for co-ordination (and thus an extended policy mix), embracing supply-side policies in addition to demand management, can also be envisaged, as suggested by several of the contributors.

Because the advent of EMU diminishes the scope for adjustment through the demand-side – given that monetary policy is 'Europeanised' and fiscal policy is constrained by the SGP – it necessarily puts more of the burden of any adjustment on the supply-side. An immediate implication is that member states have to have freedom of manoeuvre in the various domains of supply-side policy. At the same time, there is a limit to how much diversity in policy is consistent with full participation in EMU. In an area such as pension provision, in which key (and timely) decisions have evident consequences for the long-run sustainability of public finances, it can be argued that member states have to accept common objectives, as Le Cacheux shows. Similarly, if labour market reforms are central to achieving greater flexibility that lessens pressures on wage rates (see the chapters by Allsopp and by Padoan), common approaches will be warranted.

For precisely this reason, the OMC and its application to important areas of supply-side policy is regarded with suspicion: what purpose can guidelines serve (whether it is the BEPGs, the European Employment Strategy, the 'Cardiff' process or, latterly, pensions) if the rules can be avoided? The answer[4], surely, is that co-ordination can function not purely as a disciplining mechanism, but also as a means of steering policy-makers in mutually reinforcing directions and, notably, to become more receptive to alternative solutions. Many of the policy areas subject to the OMC have this property: the purpose of co-ordination of employment policy, for example, is not to discipline member states, but, by inducing them to be open and imaginative in their policy-making, to enhance the scope for the labour market to play a more effective role in adjustment. OMC can also be portrayed as a device to modernise and revitalise policy-making, if necessary by blaming the EU for demanding unpopular measures that governments would find it difficult to impose unilaterally.

Conclusions and implications for policy development

Is the system currently in place adequate for running EMU? In so far as it appears to have worked and to have survived its first real test in the form of the downturn of 2001 associated with the backwash from the US recession and the aftermath of the events of the 11th of September, the answer is a reasonably firm 'yes'. The question now, however, is whether the policy machinery is sufficiently complete and credible to cope with the longer-run challenges, especially on the supply side of the economy. In this regard, more doubts have to be expressed, not just about whether the right levers are available to be pulled, but also whether the arrangements for oversight and scrutiny of policy confer enough legitimacy.

The SGP has come in for increasing criticism since the downturn that hit the EU in 2001. These criticisms are of two kinds. To begin with, the first real test of its credibility was flunked because Ecofin refused to issue a formal warning to Germany and Portugal in 2002 when their deficits approached the 3 per cent threshold. It is a moot point whether Germany should, in fact, have been formally warned and it can be argued that the outcome – a commitment to rein in the deficit by 2004 – meant that Germany would respect the medium-term aim of the SGP, yet avoided an over-rigid application of the rules that would have been politically damaging and economically inappropriate. With hindsight and the publication of figures showing that it had breached the 3 per cent threshold, Portugal should have been 'yellow-carded'. Overall the episode reveals both a degree of pragmatic sensitivity that is probably welcome, and a fuzziness that could spell trouble.

The second strand of criticism is that the Pact's asymmetric nature means that it has a built-in deflationary bias, an altogether more intractable issue, because it can only be dealt with by more fundamental changes in its character. Options being canvassed include using cyclically adjusted budget deficits or some form of golden rule that relates the allowable deficit to public investment, as has been applied in Germany and, more recently, the UK. The trouble is, though, that any reconfiguration along such lines will involve a new phase of policy learning that could be disruptive.

Turning next to the supply-side agenda, it can be argued that the present arrangements leave much to be desired and will have to evolve considerably if processes of economic adjustment under EMU are to function more effectively, while contributing to the realisation of the 'Lisbon' aims described by Diane Coyle. The difficulties are largely political: OMC is a form of co-ordination manifestly suited to the context in which it was introduced. Suspicions about the administrative capacity of the supranational level, the fallout from the resignation of the Santer Commission and a preference for keeping policy close to home were all instrumental. Yet the paradox is that the nature of EMU places a bigger burden on the supply-side in securing economic adjustment. What constitutes flexibility in the labour market is germane, and three possible orientations can be put forward. The first is to let the market function much more freely, with less rigidity in conditions of employment and much more scope for wage adjustment. Second, flexibility can imply greater mobility, whether across sectoral or geographical boundaries A third route to flexibility is to 'invest' in labour by giving workers attributes that facilitate redeployment and help to avoid bottlenecks.

That said, what should the EES, in particular, be expected to deliver as part of the integrated post-EMU policy system? First, it ensures that employment remains firmly on the agenda, a political advantage not to be under-estimated. Second, it offers a route towards greater labour market flexibility from perspectives other than variations in wages, especially in providing for various means of enhancing the attributes of the labour force. The importance of this contribution is that it means that labour market responses are not confined to pressures that might be perceived purely negatively, such as lowering wages or lowering conditions of employment.

The way forward

As Wicks points out in the next chapter, the euro area 'is, in effect, learning by doing' in its economic management, but he cautions against expecting too much of policy co-ordination. Although there is not a consensus amongst the contributors to this volume on the eventual scope of co-ordination, their assessments point, in essence, to three options:

- Policy integration, with assignment of competence to supranational bodies, the implication of which would be the establishment of a body to fulfil the functions of *gouvernement économique*, (see, also, Jacquet and Pisani-Ferry, 2001);

- Broadly, maintenance of the status quo in which the separate arms of policy-making continue to be responsible for their respective policy areas with only informal exchanges of views and no attempts at concertation;

- A gradual consolidation of co-ordination mechanisms and channels of dialogue with a progressive formalisation of arrangements, but stopping short of major institutional development.

Still, though, there is an obvious dilemma that goes to the heart of the question of whether economic policy needs to be more extensively or formally co-ordinated: is it primarily technical or political? One view about monetary policy is that it should largely be an apolitical process in which the aim of price stability is uncontested, so that the task of policy is simply to make the correct decisions on interest rates. The Deputy-Governor of the Bank of England, Mervyn King famously summed this up in his ambition to make monetary policy 'boring'. If policy is seen as largely technical, than expert committees, such as the EFC (let alone fully fledged institutions such the ECB) – meeting in a relatively informal manner in order to ensure that the different policy actors are clear about one another's intentions and approach – are probably the pragmatic solution.

The alternative view is that how you run an economy as complex and diverse as that of the euro area is, in reality, an intensely political matter in which strategic policy choices have profound implications for the social order and there is considerable discretion in macroeconomic objectives. Certainly, as Chris Huhne shows, there is room for improvement in how economic policy in the euro area is scrutinised. The role of the European Parliament is, arguably, rather too peripheral and the influence of shadowy committees such as the Economic and Financial Committee could appear to be excessive. Both Klaus Gretschmann and Robert Boyer also highlight some of the choices that arise and remind us of the folly of believing that there is one true model of how the EU economy functions and thus how policy should be conducted.

But if more weight is given to political choices, then the need for more comprehensive policy co-ordination increases markedly. In this respect, the role of the Eurogroup is of particular interest. That it exists at all is a fluke, since it is only because three member states chose not to be part of the euro area that the Eurogroup came into being. What has become clear, however, is that its relative informality and small size as a decision-making body (one minister and one official from each member state) gives it much more scope for political input.

Procedural reforms are also at issue. In many countries (and, arguably, the Commission), the finance ministries (DG Economic and Financial Affairs) tend to be the custodians of economic orthodoxy and thus to favour stability-orientated policies, whereas labour ministries (DG Employment and Social Affairs) are apt to be regarded as more concerned with full employment aims and redistributive policies. Social affairs ministries, meanwhile, often see themselves as the guardians of the welfare state. Two sorts of solutions can be envisaged. The first would be to integrate the EES far more explicitly into the Broad Economic Policy Guidelines which would imply, almost certainly, Ecofin having the decisive role. The trade-off here is that gains in coherence would risk being offset by the loss of the creative tension of having the issue addressed by policymakers with different outlooks and priorities. The second is a variant on the notion of a *gouvernement économique*, but instead of being constituted largely as a fiscal counterpart to a powerful and integrated monetary policy, any new body should have a broader remit to orchestrate policy across a range of supply-side domains.

In conclusion, economic policy in the EU has made great strides in recent years, yet still finds itself facing uncertainties and awkward choices. On the one hand, there is a need to consolidate the policy framework sufficiently to make EMU effective and to ensure that the broader economic and social ambitions of the Union are achieved. This calls for fresh thinking about who does what in the policy framework and about the interplay between, and importance of coherence in, different policy areas. On the other hand, political imperatives combined with dismay about the conduct of some aspects of policy at the supranational level result in a reluctance to countenance the conferring of further competence on supranational bodies. As a means of resolving this dilemma, the OMC offers a promising way forward precisely because it reconciles these conflicting elements. But, in time, it may need to be reinforced by harder forms of co-ordination. With enlargement looming, the time is ripe for the EU to rise to this challenge, and our hope is that the ideas and analysis in this book will help it to do so.

Notes

[1] Interviews carried out as part of a project directed by the author

[2] During a recent visit to London, Ernst Welteke (the Bundesbank President) described how the heads of the French, German and Italian central banks wait in an anteroom while euro business is discussed in the presence of the ECB President then, in a bizarre minuet, change places with the latter when matters of national interests come on to the agenda.

[3] Notably, by Gus O'Donnell newly appointed as permanent secretary to the Treasury.

[4] I am grateful to Jacques Pelkmans and Sylvester Eijffinger for provoking me to think through these matters.

References

Alesina A., Blanchard O., Gali J., Giavazzi, F. & Uhlig H. (2001) *Defining a Macroeconomic Framework for the Euro Area: Monitoring the European Central Bank 3,* London: CEPR.

Buti, M., Roeger, W. & in't Veld, J. (2001) 'Policy conflicts and co-operation under a stability pact', *Journal of Common Market Studies*, vol. 39, no. 5, pp. 801-28.

European Commission (2002) 'Co-ordination of economic policies in the EU: a presentation of key features of the main procedures', *Euro Papers*, no. 45, Brussels: Directorate-General for Economic and Financial Affairs.

European Council (2000) 'Presidency conclusions of the Lisbon European Council', 23 & 24 March, Brussels: European Council.

Jacquet, P. & Pisani-Ferry, J. (2001) *Economic Policy Co-ordination in the Euro-Zone: What has been Achieved? What Should be Done?*, London: Centre for European Reform.

Visser, J. (2002) 'Is the European Employment Strategy the Answer?' paper presented at the NIG workshop, Utrecht, April 26th.

The Co-ordination of Economic Policies in the European Union

Nigel Wicks*

Some background

The phrase 'co-ordination of economic policies' has not hitherto been much found in the indexes of the standard economic textbooks. This is understandable since the standard treatment typically focuses upon the economics of the nation state. In that national context, the phraseology typically refers to 'economic management,' the 'policy mix' and so on. But in the context of the multi-state European Union, the phrase 'co-ordination of economic policies' is apposite because it focuses the attention of policy makers on two challenges unique to economic management in the European Union.

The first challenge reflects the fact that each member state in the European Union, even the member states in the euro area, remains responsible, to a significant degree, for its economic policies. Moreover, the combined impact of the member states' economic policies, and indeed their individual impact in the case of the larger member states, has an effect proportionately much greater than in other single currency areas. In the European Union the central budget of the Union (the Community Budget) has an insignificant effect on demand and on economic activity generally, in sharp contrast to the

---

* This paper is based on a presentation given at the Brussels Economic Forum on 2-3 May 2001.

position in federal administrations, such as the United States, Canada and Australia. Hence the emphasis in Article 99 of the Treaty on member states regarding their economic policies as a matter of common concern and the requirement to co-ordinate them within the Council.

The second challenge facing policy makers in the European Union relates to the relationship between the Union's monetary arm and its economic arm, which determines, among other policies, fiscal policy. The Treaty and its supporting texts make a sharp distinction between the monetary and economic roles, and indeed they each have their separate chapters in the Treaty. The Treaty defines clearly, too, the monetary arm, the European Central Bank (ECB) and specifies in detail its powers and responsibilities. But the Treaty is much less clear in its specification of the Union's economic arm. In fact, the economic arm has no single institutional identity corresponding to the ECB, other than the Council of Economic and Finance Ministers (Ecofin).

This institutional asymmetry between the clarity and specificity of the monetary arm and the vagueness and inchoateness of the economic arm is at the heart of the second challenge facing the Union's economic (and monetary) policy makers – the establishment of a mechanism for mutual dialogue. In the national context, such mechanisms are unnecessary, in those few cases where control of fiscal and monetary policies is still vested in the government. In the cases where the monetary arm is independent of government, it is open to the national authorities to establish either formal or informal mechanisms for dialogue.

But the European Union Treaties do not make provision for either formal or informal dialogue between the monetary and fiscal arms. During the drafting of the Maastricht Treaty, there were suggestions that the establishment of an 'economic pole' of government parallel to the monetary pole should remedy this institutional asymmetry. Such suggestions, which sometimes were presented as a move to 'economic government' (or *gouvernement économique* to use the language of its main protagonists) did not bear significant fruit, other than the creation of the annual procedure for establishing the Broad Economic Policy Guidelines.

Subsequent to the Treaty's enactment, the establishment of the Eurogroup – composed of the Finance Ministers of the member states adopting the euro – can be viewed as an attempt to resurrect, in an informal manner, the concept of an economic pole of government. The Eurogroup exists, at least so far, outside the Treaty, with neither defined responsibilities nor powers. The decision-making powers still lie with Ecofin where both euro area and non-euro area member states are represented.

It is worth emphasising that 'economic co-ordination,' as specified in the Treaty texts and as hitherto carried out in practice, does not encompass monetary policy. Monetary policy belongs to the ECB and economic policy to the Finance Ministers. The Eurogroup provides the forum for co-ordinating economic policies. It is not a forum for co-ordinating economic and monetary policies or for coming to formal, or even informal agreements, about the policy mix. It simply provides a forum for dialogue about these matters.

Three topics relating to economic co-ordination

This introduction provides the background to the discussion in this paper of three particular topics relating to the co-ordination of economic policies, namely an examination of the legislative texts on economic co-ordination, a suggestion for six tasks for economic co-ordination, and a cautionary conclusion.

The legislative texts

Scholars of medieval history will be familiar with struggles as kings and popes sought to determine the practical meaning of the verse from the Gospel according to St Matthew:

> 'Render therefore unto Caesar the things which are Caesar's; and unto God the things that are God's.'

Wars were fought and kings were excommunicated in deciding what belonged to Caesar and what belonged to God.

The ministers drafting Article 99 of the Treaty faced the same question when they had to decide which economic policy belonged to the member state and which economic policy belonged to the Community. That article makes clear that member states have economic policies of their own, though it does not specify what they are. But it also makes clear that there are economic policies of the Community, though again it does not specify what they are. The Luxembourg Resolution on Economic Policy Co-ordination of December 1997 helps to explain the reason why the need for economic co-ordination arose:

> '[T]o the extent that national economic developments have an impact on inflation prospects in the euro area, they will influence monetary conditions in that area. It is for this basic reason that the move to a single currency will require closer Community surveillance and co-ordination of economic policies...'

In short, what belongs to the member state can affect what belongs to the Community, namely the euro.

The politics of economic co-ordination are very sensitive

The politics of economic co-ordination are very sensitive; and the politics are more sensitive in some member states than in others. Some member states find it much easier to tolerate guidance from Brussels on aspects of their domestic economic policies than others. The ministers who drafted the Luxembourg Resolution were aware of all these sensitivities. The Resolution states that:

> '[E]nhanced policy co-ordination must adhere to the Treaty principle of subsidiarity, respect the prerogatives of national governments in determining their structural and budgetary policies, subject to the provisions of the Treaty and the Stability and Growth Pact...'

And the Resolution refers in relation to the wage formation process to:

> '...respect [for] national traditions and the competencies and responsibilities of the social partners...'

As an added safeguard to national sensitivities, the drafters of the Treaty made the instruments for implementing economic co-ordination 'soft law,' that is recommendations which have no binding force, rather than 'hard law,' directives, decisions and regulations, which carry legal sanctions.

There appears to be a contradiction between the use of the soft law instrument, namely a recommendation, in the principle Treaty article, Article 99, relating to economic co-ordination and the emphasis in Article 104 on hard law. Article 104 is the article that requires member states to avoid running excessive budget deficits and makes provision to levy fines on offending member states, possibly of large amounts of money. The contrast between the hard law of Article 104 and the soft law of Article 99 is more easily understandable in the light of the original purpose of Article 104. The purpose of Article 104 was to provide the powers to deter member states from running up enormous budget deficits and run the risk that other member states would have to bail them out. It is no accident that the preceding article in the Treaty contains the no-bailing out provision. It was only later, during the creation of the Stability and Growth Pact, that the excessive deficits procedure took on new prominence as an important element in economic co-ordination.

Even with Article 99's emphasis on 'soft law,' rather than 'hard law,' the politics of economic co-ordination remain extremely sensitive. So the ministers who drafted the Treaty were wise to recognise the delicate national politics. They were wise in avoiding an exact delineation of economic policy competencies between the member state and the Community. That would have been to create a rigid structure. They were wise too to leave it to events and pressures of the day to elaborate the precise details of the operation of economic co-ordination.

What should economic co-ordination be about?

So what are the events and pressures of the day, or to use the words of Hamlet '…the slings and arrows of outrageous fortune… the thousand natural shocks…' which the co-ordination of economic policies should address? In short, in today's circumstances, what are the issues facing the Union susceptible to treatment through the economic co-ordination process?

Some member state governments, which are less concerned about the domestic sensitivities of the economic co-ordination process, will answer this question with a list that amounts to virtually every aspect of economic policy. But such ambition runs the risk of alienating opinion in the other member states. It runs the risk of infringing the Community principle of 'subsidiarity,' set out in Article 5 of the Treaty, that action should be undertaken by the member states unless it can be demonstrated that better results can be achieved by action taken at the Community level. Reasons of caution and humility, described later in this chapter, also suggest putting some limit to the ambitions of economic co-ordination. So it seems prudent to confine economic co-ordination to the tasks which clearly share the characteristic of being 'of common concern,' to use the words of Article 99, to all member states, and especially to euro area members.

Six tasks which fall into this category are:

- agreeing an analysis of prospective developments, both internal and external, affecting the member states' economies;
- arising from this analysis, agreeing joint statements and presentation on economic policy matters of common and current interest, especially as they concern euro area members;
- keeping the pressure on member states with high public sector debt ratios to reduce debt levels;
- identifying prospective economic difficulties for a particular member state, especially member states in the euro area;
- conducting a dialogue with the ECB on the euro exchange rate and policy mix issues; and
- pushing forward the programme of economic reform.

Agreeing an analysis of prospective developments affecting the European economies

Agreeing an analysis of prospective developments, both internal and external, affecting the European economies is one of the core items of business of economic co-ordination. Of course, the work should not stop at analysis. Agreed policy responses, tailored to the individual circumstances of the member states, should follow from this analysis.

Statements and presentation of the Union, and especially euro area policies

It is essential for euro area representatives to send the same message about economic policy issues and to agree that message in advance. Economic co-ordination should provide the process for agreeing the public presentation and the words to use.

Prospective economic difficulties for a particular member state, especially in the euro area

A key role of the economic co-ordination process is to provide radar, scanning the horizon for future problems likely to affect individual member states, analysing economic policies in terms of the overall situation of the role of the euro. If the process identifies problems, intensive dialogue with the member state concerned would follow and the normal instruments of peer pressure should be applied, including the issue, under Article 99, of recommendations to a member state in those cases where its policies are not consistent with the broad economic guidelines.

Member states with high public sector debt ratios

There are still several member states with debt to GDP ratios above the Maastricht sixty per cent limit and some with ratios materially above that level. The process of economic co-ordination can provide a means for applying sustained persuasion on those countries, especially in those cases where they are well above the sixty per cent benchmark. The process needs to be especially active, sometimes in an unpublicised way, in member states where the government is new and there is an increased possibility that policy commitments might be entered into which conflict with the broad economic guidelines.

Conducting a dialogue with the ECB on policy mix and exchange rate issues

Strictly speaking, issues relating to the policy mix between fiscal and monetary policies are not part of the process of economic co-ordination for the simple reason that monetary policy falls outside of the process. For broadly the same reason, exchange rate policy is also not part of the process. All that properly concerns economic co-ordination is the fiscal policy element of the policy mix and the impact of fiscal policies on the euro exchange rate. Even so, the economic co-ordination process provides, for the euro area, the fiscal input into the discussion of policy mix and exchange rate issues. This link between the three subjects – economic co-ordination, policy mix and exchange rate policy – is recognised, tacitly at least, in the Treaty texts by the grouping together in the 1997 Luxembourg Resolution of material on economic co-ordination (in part I), exchange rate policy (in part II) and dialogue between the Council and the ECB (in part III). What is clear too is that the principal forum for the co-ordination of economic policies, namely the Eurogroup, provides the forum for discussion of policy mix and exchange rate issues with the ECB. It is worth adding as an aside that there is no strong evidence to suggest that so far during the life of the euro, the policy mix has been materially out of balance.

Pushing forward the programme of economic reform

The sixth task for economic co-ordination is the pushing forward of the programme of economic reform – dealing with the number one economic priority of the Union, namely to improve the efficiency of its economy. Unfortunately, the co-ordination process is ill suited to that objective. The work is detailed and painstaking and with the exception of the EMU preparations, ministerial forums in the Union have not shown themselves suited to that work. In some member states, responsibility for the subjects goes beyond the ministers who normally attend Ecofin. Even so, this is work to which Ecofin and the Eurogroup should devote more time.

Two notes of caution

The process of economic co-ordination in the European Union is still new. It is a process without precedent and which offers unique challenges. The Union is, in effect, learning by doing. So it is prudent to approach the tasks with a certain scepticism and humility. It is hard enough to manage a national economy. But the collective management of the economies of twelve member states in the euro area would be a daunting task. There is still much to learn about the linkages, 'systems effects' feedback and ripple effects between the economies. So good evidence is needed to support action or recommendations for action. The history of economic policy is littered with examples of policy action, taken for apparent good reason, only to have material, unexpected consequences.

It is important to avoid investing the concept of economic co-ordination with more than it can deliver. That was a trap that some fell into when they claimed that monetary union could work only when there was political union. There is no political union, yet there is monetary union and it is working. To predicate a successful monetary union on a working political union confused both markets and electorates. So it would be a cardinal error to claim more for economic co-ordination than it can actually deliver. Economic co-ordination is by its nature an inexact business and without the certainty of scientific rules. So those responsible for the economic co-ordination need to be ready to do their work quietly, content to be judged by results, not by rhetoric. They should bear in mind the wise words of Cicero, 'the more we are exalted, the more humbly let us bear ourselves' which might well serve as a suitable motto for the Council of Economic and Finance Ministers!

Co-ordination of economic policies in Europe: from uncertainty to apprenticeship

Robert Boyer[*]

With the arrival of euro notes and coins, there is fresh interest in how the *policy mix* is formulated in this new setting. The legal texts are clear on the conduct of monetary policy, but much less so for other facets of economic policy that remain as national competencies. It is, thus, no surprise that the start of the single currency has seen some juggling of the roles of different policy instruments.

An explanation for this institutional uncertainty is that the paradigm which underlies the Maastricht Treaty is outdated: it reflects the preoccupations of the 1980s, notably the focus on achieving monetary stability, even though this was largely attained during the period of transition to EMU (Wyplosz, 1999). This chapter examines the changes that have taken place in the way the policy mix is set, looks at the principles governing the links between monetary and fiscal policy, then at the sources of tensions that influence the overall coherence of macroeconomic policy. The chapter concludes with some suggestions for reforms aimed at achieving more effective policy-making.

---

* This chapter is an updated, abridged, but also extended essay drawn from a collective work for the Commissariat Général du Plan : *Le gouvernement économique de la Zone Euro*, with Hervé Bonnaz et Dominique Plihon, La Documentation Française, May 1999. The ideas expressed here are the sole responsibility of the author.

Fundamental changes affecting the *policy mix*

With the introduction of the euro, the asymmetry between Germany and other countries that characterised the EMS has been superseded by a new asymmetry between a single monetary policy and separately determined national fiscal policies. Under the EMS, the dominant role of the Bundesbank meant that other countries effectively had to follow its lead on interest rate decisions if they wanted to maintain stable exchange rates against the DMark. Any conflicts over the policy mix in Germany could have major repercussions for other countries, as was shown in the early 1990s when a fiscal expansion and wage pressures resulting from reunification induced a tightening of monetary policy that was inappropriate for other countries. Under EMU, the ECB has the task of assuring price stability for the union as a whole, without favouring any single country. This aim is supported by the fact that the members of the Governing Council of the ECB are bound by the Treaty not to take instructions from political authorities, and are obliged to vote in the interests of the euro area as a whole, rather than their country of origin. Thus, the policy mix will, henceforth, be the result of interactions between the single monetary policy and the national fiscal authorities, rather than German preferences, a shift that financial markets seem to have recognised.

What would happen if a shock similar to reunification were to occur? The impact on German public finances would probably be lesser and, because it would be responding to conditions in the whole euro area, the ECB would not need to tighten so much.

Two broad views on the aims of economic policies

A key question is how to organise the relationships between the different components of economic policy (Conseil d'Analyse Économique, 1998 ; Boyer 1999 ; Crouch 2000). Following Niels Thygesen (1992) and Pierre Jacquet (1998), two sorts of rationale for co-ordination of economic policies can be distinguished.

- The first is to ensure that 'public goods' such as free trade or open markets are supported. The Stability and Growth Pact (SGP) can be seen in this light, since it contributes to the viability of the euro by curbing excessive deficits.

• The second rationale is to deal with externalities resulting from policy choices in one polity that spill over to other jurisdictions. Typically, game theory is used to analyse such choices, often focusing on the trade-off between inflation and unemployment.

Two principal approaches can be distinguished.

• A first is to define rules, and is commonly used in the 'public goods' approach. Thus, the SGP stipulates when a deficit is deemed to be 'excessive' and what penalties will be imposed on the country at fault.

• Conversely, co-ordination can rely on countries using their discretionary powers in an agreed way. It is quite well suited to curbing externalities, especially where judgement is needed about the extent of the externality, making explicit rules difficult to use.

Rule-based co-ordination is, arguably, easier to implement because it is transparent and allows governments freedom of action within the prescribed limits. Thus the SGP rule that a deficit may not exceed 3 per cent of GDP means that a country below the limit can loosen fiscal policy. However, softer co-ordination may, ironically, make it more difficult to act in the same way to stimulate the economy if partner countries object because they fear spillover effects.

Potential problems in deciding on the policy mix

Many other possible problems can also be identified. First, the principles by which the ECB operates need to be clarified, while national decision-making on fiscal policy has to be reconciled with the demands from financial markets to know the overall fiscal stance of the euro area. Shortcomings in indicators mean that assessing the policy mix is not easy. The fall in the euro since its launch has also highlighted the ambiguity about the assignment of competence for its external value. The global slowdown in 2001 raised questions about how the macroeconomic policy mix impinges on reforms of labour market regulation and welfare policies, while increased international capital mobility has re-opened the question of tax harmonisation. In addition, the evidence of divergences between euro area countries in economic cycles shows how hard it is to agree on the policy mix when growth rates differ. A succession of financial crises raises questions about which level of governance should deal with prudential supervision. Finally, possible conflicts may arise between stabilisation and re-distribution aims, especially when eastern enlargement of the EU occurs.[†]

Differing views on the independence of the ECB

The independence of central banks can, using a typology suggested by Aglietta and de Boissieu (1998a), be achieved in three distinct ways: *procedural* as in the US; *instrumental* – the UK and Swedish models; or the *normative* German approach. In the first, it is the mix of deliberative processes and testing of arguments, largely through the media, that establishes credibility in the eyes of the legislature and public opinion. The second model is a principal-agent one in which governments with an overall responsibility for economic policy delegate control of monetary policy to the Central Bank. In the third approach, the Central Bank is an integral part of the constitutional order for economic management.

All three models are problematic in the EU because of the absence of a true EU level executive or of political union. The lack of a central authority also means that the EU is unable to use the sorts of fiscal stabilisers that are normal in federations, hence the search for other mechanisms (Melitz and Zumer, 1998). It follows that the independence and legitimacy of the ECB have to be based on new principles that combine aspects of these different models. The 'procedural' approach is too different from the German one to be applicable. But the normative German approach is also tricky because of the lack of political union, even though the Convention being chaired by Giscard could result in some advances. The procedural philosophy could, conceivably, be reconfigured for EMU, but its vagueness means a learning period and that it would take time to become viable. Indeed, it is only when such a system is severely tested that it really takes shape. The lack of a political counterweight is a problem for the ECB for two sets of reasons: first, marked divergences among national policies could make monetary policy more difficult to judge (Jaillet, 1998); and second, the legitimacy of the ECB could be called into question when it has to make unpopular decisions.

[†] For further details, see Boyer (1999 : table 1 p. 62-64.)

Dealing with the stability and growth procedure

When EMU was launched, the euro area countries had little room for manoeuvre in fiscal policy because of the Maastricht convergence criteria and the demands of the SGP. The degree of budgetary 'consolidation' required in different countries was, however, very uneven (Buti and Giudice, 2002). The fiscal position of several countries remains delicate, so that the risk of budgetary problems is not negligible. Two possibilities are:

- A general worsening of budgetary balances caused by an economic slowdown affecting the whole euro area. Such an outcome could arise, first, because steady growth is by no means guaranteed, and, second, because convergence of economic cycles makes a synchronised downturn more likely.

- Fiscal problems resulting from an asymmetric shock affecting a large country, either because it has trouble curbing public expenditure or because of internal political circumstances.

The SGP rules allow some leeway (as explained in Box 1 in the introduction of this volume) for governments facing adjustment problems, especially if they can demonstrate that they face exceptional circumstances, and the pact also allows them time to respond before sanctions are imposed (Eichengreen and Wyplosz, 1998). Moreover, the Ecofin Council has to agree by qualified majority to impose sanctions. Yet despite the scope for flexibility in implementation, the SGP commits governments and clearly exerts a powerful influence on their behaviour. Consequently, fiscal laxity could lead to two sorts of tensions:

- *Financial market tensions*: issuers of sovereign debt could see a degradation of their credit ratings. The resulting impact on interest rates payable on government debt is likely to be magnified under EMU, leading to an intensification of competition between issuers of debt, exerting a discipline on countries. With spreads only reflecting credit risk, rather than currency risk as in the past, investors will grade public debt like any other bonds and market practitioners analysing the bonds will take account not only of the public deficit, but of the broader fiscal policy stance (Waysand, 1998). In addition, market concerns about the euro may also be greater if fiscal problems are evident in several important euro area countries.

- *Tensions between the ECB, Ecofin and Member States* when excessive deficits arise: the ECB is bound to act if such deficits put at risk the credibility of its strategy to assure price stability. Several responses by the ECB and its counterparts can be envisaged. A first is a game of 'chicken' in which the ECB demands curbs on deficits, while the fiscal authorities call for cuts in interest rates to stimulate growth and reduce debt costs. Such a non-co-operative solution – waiting to see who blinks first – is the least attractive, because it turns the ECB into a scapegoat and could undermine market confidence. The criticisms of Germany and Portugal in 2002 illustrate these tensions, even though a formal warning was not issued, and highlight the difficulty of distinguishing structural and cyclical deficits in a context of global slowdown.

The awkward question of exchange rate management

Under the Treaty, competence for exchange rate policy is shared between the ECB and the Council, a division that can also be expected to engender tensions. Although the single currency manifestly simplifies matters compared with previous arrangements, it also raises new challenges about the external value of the euro, about which countries may have divergent views.

According to article 109 of the Treaty, the Council is responsible for negotiating formal exchange rate arrangements with third countries and the international institutions, as well as for giving broad guidance to the ECB on exchange rate policy, implying joint decision-making between the ECB and the Council. But in practice, the Council has few powers (Rolland-Piègue, 1998), because the ECB holds sway over the principal policy instrument – the interest rate – while article 109 gives the ECB the right to ignore Council recommendations if it perceives a threat to price stability: its core mandate.

Consequently, the scope for conflict between the ECB and the Council remains, even though the former seems to hold most of the cards. Differing productive structures among the twelve euro area economies mean that exchange rate movements will have markedly different effects (Maurel, 1999). Potential conflicts can also be envisaged in international fora, not least because the Treaty is vague on international representation of the euro. Whatever solution is found, it is bound to be difficult to reconcile the positions of diverse Community institutions and national interests.

Contrary to initial expectations, the euro fell sharply relative to the dollar between its inception and the autumn of 2000 and only moved back towards parity in the summer of 2002, despite fluctuating trends in the real economies on both sides of the Atlantic. There is, as yet, no consensus based on fundamentals (e.g. inflation, interest rates and growth prospects) on why the euro fell so much, but there is evidence that confusion over the policy mix and exchange rate policy may have played a part.

It may, therefore, be worth clarifying the importance accorded to the exchange rate within monetary policy and how it influences decisions. Does the ECB have a medium term target for the exchange rate as well as its threshold for inflation? If so, how transparent is the target and does the ECB have any plans to communicate its strategy? A more awkward issue is the exchange rate regime: between the leading currencies, there has to be both flexibility and management (i.e. a managed float). So far, the indications are that the ECB is prepared to let the currency float freely, but to react when movements become excessive.

Spillovers between monetary policy and prudential supervision

A properly functioning banking system is central to modern capitalist economies, especially in administering payments systems. Financial intermediaries also play a pivotal role in the transmission of monetary policy. Yet the ECB has only a minimal role in prudential supervision of credit institutions, with the main responsibilities left to member states – using their own methods – in accordance with the principle of subsidiarity. The rationale for this division of labour is that national supervisors are more familiar with their 'clients' and can, therefore, oversee them more effectively.

Some economists fear that this decentralised system for supervision will soon find itself at odds with change in the EU's banking and financial sectors (Aglietta et de Boissieu, 1998b). Once the expected cross-border consolidation of the industry occurs, resulting in pan-European networks, financial intermediaries will cease to have a single national base. Bank defaults would no longer affect a single NCB, but be spread across several, resulting in liquidity crises that accentuate systemic risks. Future stock market crashes could, similarly, reverberate across the euro area. Who would be the lender of last resort in these circumstances?

Centralised supervision would not, however, be universally welcomed (Lannoo, 1998) and enhanced co-operation between national supervisors could solve most problems. It may, moreover, be too soon to seek an EU-wide system for lending in the last resort if only because of the ambiguity with which central bankers like to treat the matter, although the implication is that improved exchange of information will be required (Jaillet, 1998). As regards the supervision of pan-European conglomerates, procedures already exist through the EU's Banking Supervision Committee and the Bank for International Settlements.

What this question highlights is how difficult it can be to choose between rules, co-ordination or discretionary action, and the need for conceptual and empirical analysis. Radically different answers may be appropriate in different settings.

Structural reforms

Structural policies are believed to be essential to complement macroeconomic policy in the EU context, as has been stressed repeatedly in pronouncements by the ECB and by other commentators (Bureau, 1998). Some argue that the absence of inter-regional transfer mechanisms (unlike other monetary unions) deprives the euro area of a tool for dealing with structural problems. Others stress the need for far-reaching reforms to improve the functioning of markets, notably by removing competitive distortions.

Tax harmonisation is often mentioned as one of the key priorities for the euro area for two main reasons: first, the disappointing progress under this domain of single market initiatives; and, second, the likelihood that tax competition will intensify with the single currency (le Cacheux, 1998). Some progress has been made on this front, but it is likely to be a long haul.

Industrial relations and the scope of wage bargaining are also increasingly under the microscope. Collective bargaining has to fit into the monetary stability framework adopted by the ECB, which will be challenging for those countries which have not been accustomed to this approach. The aim can, moreover, be achieved in diverse ways, ranging from national pacts to complete decentralisation of bargaining, with an array of intermediate styles (Beffa, Boyer et Touffut, 1999). It can be argued that these relationships are so critical that, however difficult, co-ordination along the lines envisaged in the conclusions of the 1999 Cologne European Council is vital.

Persistent differences in monetary transmission mechanisms

It is important to know how the single monetary policy will be transmitted to the real economy. If economies respond very differently to the same interest rate movement, it would be much more difficult to achieve an appropriate EU-level policy mix. The many studies that have examined this question have had to deal with a changing context, notably changes in product and labour markets and financial innovation, and they have often had contradictory results. In addition, some channels of transmission have ceased to exist: exchange rate movement, interest rate disparities and attendant risk premia, although these had, in any case, faded in recent years. A survey of recent studies by the OECD (1998) nevertheless found few differences between the euro area economies in their responses to interest rate changes. This suggests that the impact of monetary policy on the real economy will be broadly similar in the main European economies.

These results do, however, have to interpreted with caution, because they depend, above all, on the character of financial systems, which remain quite heterogeneous across the euro area. In particular, the relative importance of banking and the balance between short- and long-term debt vary considerably. Where the prominence of securities markets relative to bank credit is greater, the reaction to monetary policy will be greater and more immediate. Other factors which contribute to national differences include the split between variable rate and fixed rate lending and the degree of indebtedness of households. In parallel, wage setting mechanisms and the links between prices and wage rates make a difference.

Findings for the early years of the euro suggest that growth rates, inflation and unemployment have converged less than expected (European Economy, 2001). It follows that member states need to have instruments capable of dealing with imbalances in their economies. This argues for a degree of decentralisation in economic policy-making provided that there are no significant externalities.

Rules, co-ordination or discretion?

Two broad questions can be posed about economic policy: how should competencies be allocated between tiers of government; and, where there are significant spillovers, how should these be dealt with in the policy system. The answer will depend on the salience of public goods and on the extent of interdependencies across borders and policy domains. The accompanying table summarises the problems and potential solutions, pointing to the implications for more extensive policy co-ordination. The following issues emerge as critical:

- Across the economic policy spectrum, there are difficulties associated with both the management of trans-national public goods and of externalities between domains, encompassing differing tiers and agencies of governance.

- If the main concern is about public goods, particularly within a well-defined policy area with little backwash on to others, the framing of rules is a good way forward. The excessive deficit procedures are a case in point, because they help to bolster the credibility of the ECB, helped by the no bail out clause in the Treaty. Cross-border multiplier effects of public spending can be handled in two ways. The first, if one has faith in the open method of co-ordination (Rodrigues, 2002), is peer review of national budgets and longer-term surveillance of spending programmes. The alternative is to devise hard rules about the medium- and long-term trends in public spending so as to ensure that national plans are compatible.

- If, however, it is linkages between policy domains that predominate, the only option is to use exchange of information to inform policy choices in the hope that such discourse will encourage explicit policy co-ordination. This is especially true of the overlaps between European monetary policy, national fiscal policies and wage setting behaviour, the more so when the last of these can function at national, regional, sectoral or company levels (Maurice, 1999). The outcome of dialogue could be agreement on coherent targets for interest rates, the fiscal stance and wage settlements.

- Equally, one cannot ignore the importance of discretionary policies in response to domestic social or political imperatives, or to fluctuations in the economic cycle or financial markets. Policy-making is likely to be improved if discourse and 'soft' methods of concerting and co-ordinating policy are allowed to complement hard rules. It is in this context that a case can be made for consolidating the different forms of economic governance into some form of 'gouvernement économique' for the euro area (Boyer, 1999 ; Boyer et Dehove, 2001a ; 2001b).

• These considerations bring us to a key topic, namely the long-term determinants of growth. The movements in the euro exchange rate *vis-à-vis* the dollar are often interpreted in terms of the technological gap between the old and the new world, thought to have been the main factor behind the difference in growth rates observed in the 1990s. This highlights the importance of R&D policy in which there are both public good arguments and cross-border externalities to take into account, not least because trans-national networks facilitate better returns on R&D outlays. In this regard, the EU is handicapped in two ways. First, most member states devote a lower proportion of their GDP than the US to R&D, a deficiency which might justify a target for enhancing the research effort. Second, specialists in technical change stress that the creation of networks around nodes of excellence is essential if Europe is to become more competitive in certain new technologies (Soete, 2002). Moreover, it could help to promote a form of economic growth that is consistent with the European social model (Esping-Andersen, 2002 ; Atkinson, 2002 ; Boyer, 1998b ; 2000).

From these perspectives, it is not enough to rely on Treaty provisions alone to shape the conduct and co-ordination of economic policy. Instead, it is incumbent on the various actors to review their strategies in the light of experience and to take account of inter-linkages. The history of European integration suggests that this is how institutional development proceeds (Moravcsik, 1998).

1999-2002: Towards a period of apprenticeship for economic policy actors

Since the launch of the euro, much has been learned about the imbalances and difficulties likely to undermine the quality of euro area economic policy. An early fear was that there would be a deflationary bias in monetary policy, but the return to steady growth, followed by the downturn in the US economy seems to have elicited a pragmatic response. This suggests that the learning process has led the authorities to look beyond a narrow focus on the 'public good' of the single currency to make allowance for inter-actions between different areas of economic policy. Questions arise about the compatibility of tax systems, how to speed-up adoption of new technologies, means of

Table 1: An eclectic approach to problem and solutions

PROBLEMS AND SOLUTIONS / POLICY AREA	NATURE OF PROBLEM		SOLUTIONS		
	Public good	Externalities	Rules	Co-ordination/Concertation	Discretionary measures
Single currency	Price stability	Impact of lower interest rates on public finances	Keeping inflation below a threshold	Among the euro-12	Damaging to credibility and transparency
National budgets	National public capital	• The size of the public deficit affects the euro's credibility • Effects on the economic cycle of other countries	• The excessive deficits provisions • Rules governing short – to medium-term spending plans	• Concertation between ECB & finance ministries collectively • Concertation with other finance ministries	• Justified by unpredictable events • Allow case by case responses
Prudential supervision	Financial stability	The effectiveness of monetary policy depends on the robustness of the financial system	Prudential controls applied at national level but decided by the BIS	Needed if there is cross-border financial integration	Support from a lender of last resort, but danger from moral hazard
Taxation	Social justice	Attractiveness of low tax countries	European-level taxation of mobile factors of production	Tax harmonisation	Either national or EU level responses to emerging problems
The welfare state	Social cohesion at the national level	Danger of a 'race to the bottom'	Host country control instead of home country	The open method of co-ordination	Ad-hoc solutions to changes in intra-European mobility
Industrial relations	Industrial peace and fair wage settlements	• Danger of a 'race to the bottom' • Effects on wage dynamics and thus on price inflation	• Common cross-border rules (e.g. collective agreements) • Decentralised labour laws	• Social dialogue at the European or trans-national level • Cologne process: concertation between the ECB, finance ministries and the social partners	• Shifts as a result of disputes or 'euro-strikes' • Recognition of ECB objectives in wage setting
Research	Advances in knowledge	Positive *spillovers* from research networks	A target for the share of R&D as a proportion of GDP	Fostering of networks around centres of excellence	Decisions case by case on research programmes

comparing employment policies and how to reform welfare systems to anticipate the effects of ageing (Rodrigues, 2002).

An answer may be to revisit the suggestions made in the late 1990s (Lafontaine and Strauss-Kahn, 1999) and reiterated since by Jacquet and Pisani-Ferry (2000) for concertation leading eventually to explicit co-ordination between the ECB, finance ministers and the social partners. Within this framework:

- *The social partners* would be charged with delivering wage increases that matched productivity gains, such that labour costs were broadly constant, thereby avoiding higher interest rate increases by the ECB. Wage negotiations would, thus, play a central role in assuring price stability, constituting a significant advance on traditional monetarism.

- *Finance ministries* would be responsible for keeping public spending in line with the growth in the economy, for seeking to cut taxes in periods of rapid growth and ensuring sufficient public investment targeted at long-term growth. In practice, these measures would keep deficits under control while providing room for manoeuvre in dealing with asymmetric shocks.

- *The ECB* would be expected to adopt a balanced strategy that avoids deflation as well as inflation. This would be more easily achieved if excesses were avoided in either wage increases or fiscal deficits. In such circumstances, the ECB could play a central role in countering symmetric shocks, as the Fed does (Muet and Pisani-Ferry, 1995), and the system overall would avoid the failures of co-ordination in the policy mix that characterised the 1990s (Muet, 1995; Muet, 1998).

It is conceivable that a 'virtuous cycle' could be created in which price stability is associated not with slower growth, but with a sustained improvement in medium term prospects. The SGP could, then, be superseded by monitoring of medium-term spending plans (von Hagen and Harden, 1994) without the need for a 3 per cent rule that prevents action in exceptional circumstances.

Conclusion

This chapter has tried to show that despite the Treaty and the successful introduction of the euro, there is still much to discuss about the architecture of economic policy in Europe. Indeed, developments since 1999 have prompted some rethinking. To take just one example, the assumption that the euro would be a strong currency has been proved wrong – even though with hindsight the fall in the currency was an advantage because it helped to support growth in the period during which the euro was launched. It is, nevertheless, important to draw lessons for the policy mix from this gap between expectation and outcome.

A first lesson is that there are both new and varied inter-relationships that policy actors have to assimilate. A second is that there is a range of possible approaches to dealing with the European 'public interest' and the interdependencies between economic policy domains: rules, co-ordination, co-operation and discretionary action are all options, though they will often be applied simultaneously. A third conclusion is that policy 'apprenticeship' is vital, yet can readily be accommodated within existing procedures as defined by the Treaty.

Nonetheless, it would be wrong to overlook the potential benefits of a review of the policy machinery (Quermone, 1999 ; Boyer et Dehove, 2001a ; 2001b). Many of the issues that are only partially dealt with by the open method of co-ordination would be settled more convincingly if there were a *gouvernement économique* of the euro area, and there are pressures to introduce one. Should Europe not be developing its institutions to enable it to meet the competitive challenges from the US and Asia? With the accession of new members to the EU, should there not be a more radical overhaul than in the past of the policy system? Finally, in response to popular concern, is it not time to clarify the allocation of competencies?

These are all reasons to revitalise the approaches to economic policy both at EU and national levels.

References

Aglietta, M. & de Boissieu, C. (1998a) 'La responsabilité de la future Banque centrale européenne', in *Coordination européenne des politiques économiques*, Conseil d'Analyse Économique, Paris: La Documentation Française.

Aglietta, M. & de Boissieu, C. (1998b) 'Problèmes prudentiels' in *Coordination européenne des politiques économiques*, rapport au Conseil d'Analyse Économique, Paris: La Documentation Française.

Atkinson, T. (2002) 'Reassessing the Fundamentals: Social Inclusion and the European Union', forthcoming in *Journal of Common Market Studies*, 40.4.

Beffa, J-L., Boyer, R. & Touffut J-P (1999) 'Les relations salariales en France: État, entreprises, marchés financiers', *Notes de la Fondation Saint Simon*, no. 107, Juin.

Boyer, R. (1998a) 'An essay on the political and institutional deficits of the Euro. The unanticipated fallout of the European Monetary Union', in *Couverture Orange CEPREMAP*, no. 9813, p. 125, August.

Boyer, R. (1998b) 'Réformes des procédures européennes et croissance', *Rapport du Conseil d'Analyse Économique*, no. 27, *Questions européennes*, Pierre J. & Pisani-Ferry, J., et al. (2000), pp. 72-108, Paris: La Documentation Française.

Boyer, R. (2000) 'The Unanticipated fallout of European Monetary Union: The Political and Institutional Deficits of the Euro', in Crouch, C. (Ed.) *After the Euro*, pp. 24-88, Oxford: Oxford University Press.

Boyer, R. (sous la présidence) (1999) *Le gouvernement économique de la zone euro*, Paris: La Documentation Française.

Boyer, R. & Dehove, M. (2001a) 'Du 'gouvernement économique' au gouvernement tout court', *Critique Internationale*, no. 11, pp. 179-195, April.

Boyer, R. & Dehove, M. (2001b) 'Théories de l'intégration européenne: entre gouvernance et gouvernement', *La Lettre de la Régulation*, no. 38, pp. 1-3, September, Paris.

Bureau, D. (1998) 'Coordination européenne des politiques économiques, Monnaie unique, et politiques structurelles', in *Coordination européenne des politiques économiques*, rapport au Conseil d'Analyse Économique, Paris: La Documentation Française.

Buti, M. & Giudice, G. (2002) 'Maastricht's Fiscal Rules at Ten: An Assessment', mimeograph, March 25, European Commission.

Conseil d'Analyse Économique (1998) *Coordination européenne des politiques économiques*, no. 5, Paris: La Documentation Française.

Economie Européenne (2001) *Les grandes orientations de politique économique de 2001*, no. 72, Bruxelles: Commission Européenne.

Eichengreen, B. & et Wyplosz, C. (1998) 'The Stability Pact: More than a Minor Nuisance?', *Economic Policy*, vol. 26, April.

Esping Andersen, G. (2002) 'A New European Social Model for the 21st Century?', in Rodrigues, M. J. (ed.) *The new Knowledge Economy in Europe. A strategy for international competitiveness with social cohesion*, Adelshot: Edward Elgar.

Hagen, J. von Harden, I. (1994) 'National budget process and fiscal performance', *European Economic Reports and Studies*, no. 3.

Jacquet, P. (1998) 'L'Union monétaire et la coordination des politiques macroéconomiques', *Conseil d'Analyse Économique*, no. 5, pp. 35-46, Paris: La Documentation Française.

Jaillet P. (1998) 'Stratégies de politique monétaire : quelques enseignements du passé récent et pistes pour l'avenir', *Revue Économique*, vol. 49, no. 3, Mai.

Lafontaine, O. & Strauss-Kahn, D. (1999) 'Tirer le meilleur parti de l'Euro', *Le Monde*, 15, janvier, pp.1, 13.

Lannoo K. (1998) 'Financial Supervision in EMU', mimeograph, 29 décembre, Brussels: Centre for European Policy Studies (CEPS).

Le Cacheux, J. (2000) 'Les dangers de la concurrence fiscale et sociale en Europe', *Conseil D'analyse Économique*, no. 27, *Questions européennes*, pp. 41-56, Paris: La Documentation Française.

Maurel, F. (sous la présidence de) (1999) *Marché unique, monnaie unique : trois scénarios pour une nouvelle géographie unique de l'Europe*, rapport du groupe 'Géographie économique', Commissariat général du Plan, Paris: La Documentation Française.

Maurice, J. (sous la présidence de) (1999) *Emploi, négociation collective, protection sociale: vers quelle Europe sociale?*, Rapport du groupe 'Europe Sociale', Commissariat général du Plan, Paris: La Documentation Française.

Mélitz, J. & Zumer, F. (1998) 'Redistribution régionale et stabilisation par le gouvernement central', *Économie internationale*, La revue du CEPII, 3ème trimestre, no. 75, pp. 3-31.

Moravcsik, A. (1998) *The Choice for Europe*, Ithaca: Cornell University Press.

Muet, P-A. (1995) 'Ajustements macroéconomiques, stabilisation et coordination en Union monétaire', *Revue d'Économie Politique*, 105 (5), Septembre-Octobre, pp. 739-777.

Muet, P-A. (1998) 'Déficit de croissance et défaut de coordination: une analyse rétrospective', in *Coordination européenne des politiques économiques*, rapport au Conseil d'Analyse Économique, Paris: La Documentation Française.

Muet, P-A. & Pisani-Ferry, J. (1995) 'Macroeconomic Policy Co-ordination in EMU', papier préparé pour le Séminaire franco-britannique sur l'Euro, 15 février, Paris.

OCDE (1998) 'Enjeux de politique monétaire et budgétaire dans la zone Euro', *Perspectives Économiques de l'OCDE*, no. 64, Décembre.

Quermone, J-L. (sous la présidence de) (1999) *L'Union européenne en quête d'institutions légitimes et efficaces*, Rapport Commissariat Général du Plan, Paris: La Documentation Française.

Rodrigues, M. J. (ed.) (2002) *The new Knowledge Economy in Europe. A strategy for international competitiveness with social cohesion*, Adelshot: Edward Elgar.

Rolland-Piègue, É. (1998) 'La politique de change de l'Euro', Ronéotypé préparé pour le groupe 'Coordination des politiques macroéconomiques', Commissariat général du Plan.

Soete, L. (2002) 'The Challenges and the Potential of the Knowledge-Based Economy in a Globalized World', in Rodrigues M. J. (ed.) *The new Knowledge Economy in Europe. A strategy for international competitiveness with social cohesion*, Adelshot: Edward Elgar.

Thygesen, N. (1992) 'Coordination of national policies', in Newman, P., Milgate, M. & Eatwell, J. (Eds.) *The New Palgrave Dictionary of Money and Finance*, vol. I, pp. 458-461, London: Macmillan.

Waysand, C. (1998) 'Comment les marchés financiers évalueront-ils la conduite des politiques budgétaires nationales en UEM?', Ronéotypé préparé pour le groupe 'Coordination des politiques macroéconomiques', Commissariat général du Plan, Septembre.

Wyplosz C. (1999) 'Economic Policy Coordination in EMU : Strategies and Institutions', *Mimeograph of Graduate Institute of International Studies*, Geneva, presented at the German-French Economic Forum in Bonn, 12 janvier.

On Macro-economic Policy Co-ordination in EMU

Otmar Issing[*]

Introduction

The formation of Economic and Monetary Union (EMU) has created a framework for economic policy-making in Europe which is unique in history. While the single monetary policy is oriented towards a union-wide objective, namely the maintenance of price stability, the other policy areas – involving fiscal and wage policies – largely remain the competence of national governments and other national actors, such as the social partners.

Against this background, calls for enhanced macroeconomic policy co-ordination between monetary policy, on the one hand, and fiscal and wage policies, on the other hand, have come about as a result of the perception that the new institutional framework in EMU places constraints on the different policies. More specifically, it is argued that these constraints could be alleviated by setting the available policy instruments in a co-ordinated manner in order to achieve a macro-economic policy-mix at the euro area level that is conducive to higher growth and employment.[1]

The central message I wish to convey here, however, is that there are no convincing arguments in favour of attempts to co-ordinate macro-economic policies *ex ante* in order to achieve an overall policy mix favourable to growth

* I would like to thank Günter Coenen for his valuable contribution. This chapter was originally published in Vol 40.2 of the *Journal of Common Market Studies* and is reproduced by kind permission of Blackwell Publishers Ltd.

and employment. On the contrary, attempts that extend beyond the informal exchange of views and information give rise to the risk of confusing the specific roles, mandates and responsibilities of the policies in question. Thereby they reduce the transparency of the overall economic policy framework for the general public and tend to prevent the individual policy-makers from being held accountable.

Instead I shall argue that national governments and autonomous social partners should design and implement the policies for which they are responsible bearing in mind the overall stability framework provided for in the Maastricht Treaty and the secondary legislation, including the Stability and Growth Pact. As a result sustainable and prudent fiscal policies and moderate developments in wage costs, which take into account the interdependencies between the latter and the stability-oriented single monetary policy, will already go a long way towards providing favourable conditions for economic growth and employment. Obviously, if national governments and social partners take the single monetary policy's credible commitment to maintain price stability as given when deciding upon their own actions, this will lead to implicitly co-ordinate policy outcomes ex post, while at the same time limiting policy conflicts and overall economic uncertainty.[2]

Because macro-economic policies cannot resolve the underlying structural causes of Europe's growth and employment problems, I shall stress the importance of policies aimed at the micro level. Such policies have the necessary instruments to tackle the roots of the structural problems, namely rigidities in the goods and labour markets, and are thus responsible for ensuring higher growth and more favourable employment prospects in Europe.

The discussion is organised as follows. I shall first point to the limited scope for macro-economic policy co-ordination in general. Then I shall briefly review the principal provisions of the Maastricht Treaty and the Stability and Growth Pact arguing that the clear assignment of responsibilities therein substitutes for explicit co-ordination among policy-makers. Further I shall elaborate on the particular ways in which the Eurosystem's single monetary policy contributes to the stable policy framework in EMU. A brief discussion of the role of structural reforms will conclude.

The limited scope for macro-economic policy co-ordination

The calls for policy co-ordination are based on the idea that individual policies, which affect one another, should take one another's objectives and actions into account. Partial neglect of these interdependencies – so-called externalities or spillover effects – would lead to a sub-optimal outcome of policies which policy-makers could improve upon through an agreement on a joint setting of their instruments to get closer to their own preferred policy choices. This idea appears to be an attractive and self-evident proposition and is true, almost by definition, for the simple two-player models which were initially used in the literature on optimal policy co-ordination to analyse the welfare gains of moving from a non co-operative 'Nash' equilibrium towards a co-operative 'bargaining' equilibrium.

In the course of the last two decades the analytical underpinnings of optimal policy co-ordination have been deepened and clarified, and elaborate efforts at empirical estimation of the potential welfare gains from policy co-ordination have been undertaken.[3] At least at the macro level, however, empirical estimates of the size of the gains from policy co-ordination have been found to be modest and sometimes of uncertain sign.[4] Moreover, a number of lessons can be drawn from the literature which indicate that there are already severe conceptual problems limiting the scope of policy co-ordination for the purpose of practical policy-making.

From a practical perspective, co-ordination of different policies creates serious problems with regard to gathering and processing all relevant information in an effective and timely manner. Traditionally, the literature on macro-economic policy co-ordination has been concerned with spillovers arising from short-run policy actions in the context of stabilisation policies. To pursue such policies effectively requires, first, to identify the shocks that affect the economic situation and, second, to agree on a proper macro-economic model that allows quantifying how both the shocks and the contemplated policy actions impact on economic variables over the relevant policy horizon.[5] Practical experience shows that it is already difficult to correctly identify the nature of economic shocks, leaving aside the need to arrive at a common understanding of their propagation over time and the possible spillovers of joint policy actions. As a result attempts to co-ordinate policy actions seems particularly prone to the well-known recognition and decision lags of policy-making rendering the timely agreement on the appropriate joint actions in practice almost impossible.

Even more importantly, the calls for policy co-ordination generally disregard the political-economy context of practical policy-making and, therefore, an essential component of reality. Policy co-ordination among several policy-makers generally gives rise to the risk of distorting the individual policy-makers' incentives to choose appropriate policies by confusing their individual responsibilities and reducing their ability to be held accountable.[6] In the worst case scenario, if everyone is regarded as being responsible for everything, no one will take responsibility for anything. Furthermore, the actual implementation of co-ordinated policy decisions in the jurisdictions of the individual policy-makers may suffer from a lack of appropriate enforcement mechanisms, which, *inter alia*, would help to contain free-riding behaviour by individual policy-makers.

For all these reasons possible welfare gains from optimal policy co-ordination appear to be of second-order importance relative to improving a common understanding, providing adequate incentives and establishing appropriate enforcement mechanisms. To the extent that the severe information, incentive and enforcement problems decisively undermine the practicability of policy co-ordination, one may therefore wonder how these problems can be alleviated, or – more important – how individual policy-makers can take into account one another's objectives and actions from the outset so that policy co-ordination would, in fact, be largely unnecessary.

I am convinced that designing the appropriate institutions lies at the heart of the answer to this question. Let us consider the issue of policy co-ordination being conditional on an initial assignment of objectives and instruments to individual policy-makers. Calls for policy co-ordination would, in this case, be based on the assumption that this kind of assignment does not appropriately reflect the interdependencies of the policy-makers' objectives and actions. By contrast, if there is already an *efficient* initial assignment in place, which does take into account the individual policy-makers' objectives and actions, and if the policy-makers' responsibilities are clearly defined, calls for policy co-ordination, which would be fraught with the aforementioned problems, would not be necessary.[7] To put it simply, an efficient initial assignment of objectives and instruments, together with a clear division of responsibilities, will achieve *implicitly* co-ordinated outcomes *ex post* and thereby largely substitute the need for *explicitly* co-ordinated policies later on.

In the euro area, the Maastricht Treaty already provides for such an efficient assignment of objectives with a sound and clear allocation of responsibilities to the individual policy-makers thus making the scope for additional policy co-ordination rather limited. This assignment clearly defines the European Central Bank's role and provides rules for the other policy-makers' contributions to economic stability.

Responsibilities under the 'Maastricht Assignment'

The central legal basis for economic policy co-ordination within EMU is specified in Article 99 (ex 103) of the Maastricht Treaty, which states that 'Member States shall regard their economic policies as a matter of common concern and shall co-ordinate them within the Council.' On the basis of this principle, the framework for the definition of overall economic policy objectives and orientations is provided by the 'Broad Economic Policy Guidelines' adopted by the Council each year.

With regard to monetary and fiscal policies, the assignment of responsibilities is defined by the Maastricht Treaty and the Stability and Growth Pact respectively. The Treaty has assigned the maintenance of price stability as the primary objective to the single monetary policy under Article 105. Without prejudice to its primary objective, the single monetary policy shall support the general economic policies of the European Community. The Stability and Growth Pact provides guidelines for fiscal discipline at the national level by strengthening the excessive deficit procedure of the Treaty and by prescribing sanctions for breaches of the 3 per cent limit of the deficit-to-GDP ratio. It also specifies a commitment to achieving medium-term budgetary positions 'close to balance or in surplus' and incorporates multilateral surveillance procedures and the exchange of information in conjunction with medium-term stability programmes submitted by national governments.

Assigning the overriding objective of price stability to the single monetary policy is a prominent example of how to realise the benefits of the basic division of responsibilities provided for by the Maastricht Treaty. The single monetary policy – safeguarded by an independent central bank – enhances the credibility of monetary policy, increases its transparency and also facilitates its accountability. Similarly, the Stability and Growth Pact provides the right incentives for the conduct of sound and disciplined fiscal policies across all national governments, while preserving sufficient room for manoeuvre for the operation of automatic stabilisers and prudent anti-cyclical policies without infringing the ceiling of the deficit-to-GDP ratio.[8]

While the Maastricht Treaty and the Stability and Growth Pact make provisions for monetary and fiscal policies – either in the form of the single monetary policy or in the form of disciplinary rules for national governments – wage developments largely remain the result of bargaining among autonomous social partners at the national level. It is evident, however, that the social partners – sometimes contrary to their own perceptions – would act in their own interest by ensuring that price stability and a high level of employment are compatible. Given the fact that the relationship between wage developments, productivity growth and price stability plays an important role in this respect, real wage increases, which do not exceed trend productivity growth, will facilitate the maintenance of price stability and simultaneously promote employment. Obviously, in times of high unemployment, when there is a need to stimulate job creation, employment-oriented wage settlements should not fully exploit productivity increases. Moreover, wage settlements should account for sectoral and regional differences in productivity and labour market conditions. With regard to the role of national governments in this context, modest wage settlements in the public sector should set an example for wage developments in the whole economy that are conducive to a high level of employment and consistent with price stability.

If all policy areas concerned respect the aforementioned allocation of objectives and responsibilities and act accordingly, they will already be making the best possible contribution to the Community objectives as provided for by the 'Broad Economic Policy Guidelines.' Of course, an open exchange of views and information between individual policy actors – without any commitment or mandate to take and implement joint decisions – will assist the overall outcome if it manages to improve the understanding of the objectives and responsibilities of the respective policy areas and does not dilute accountability. This exchange of information will be facilitated, for instance, by the 'Macroeconomic Dialogue' under the European Employment Pact, which was endorsed at the Cologne European Council meeting in June 1999.

Any form of dialogue, however, should clearly be distinguished from an attempt to co-ordinate macro-economic policies *ex ante*, which would give rise to the information, incentive and enforcement problems mentioned above. Indeed, given the lack of mutual enforcement mechanisms, *ex ante* co-ordination among the different policy actors would tend to blur the fundamental responsibilities of the respective policy areas under the Treaty. This, in turn, would distort incentives, reduce the accountability of individual policy actors and ultimately increase uncertainty about the policy framework.

While the ECB is engaged in a regular exchange of views and information with other policy actors in fulfilling its mandate, there are clear limits to the forms such a dialogue can take. Any dialogue must respect the principle of central bank independence enshrined in the Treaty and must be consistent with the Treaty's allocation of responsibilities. In particular, any form of *ex ante* co-ordination involving the ECB that would entail some form of commitment regarding monetary policy which could compromise the maintenance of price stability is not compatible with the Treaty.

Against this background, the following section will elaborate on the particular ways in which the single monetary policy contributes to non-inflationary growth and a high level of employment within the overall stability framework established under the Treaty.

The contribution of the single monetary policy

The single monetary policy is responsible for maintaining price stability in the euro area as laid down in the Maastricht Treaty. To this end, the Eurosystem has adopted a medium-term-oriented monetary policy strategy which is forward-looking and enables prompt action to be taken in order to address any potential threats to price stability. Moreover, the Eurosystem's definition of price stability gives a clear quantification of how its mandate will be interpreted by the Governing Council of the ECB which, in turn, will enhance the transparency and effectiveness of the single monetary policy.

Theory and empirical evidence confirm that there is no long-term trade-off between price stability and economic growth. Attempting to use monetary policy to gear economic activity above a sustainable level will, in the long run, simply lead to rising inflation, and not to higher economic growth. In the same vein, monetary policy should not try to fine-tune economic developments. An activist monetary policy, which does not take into account both the long and variable time lags of its transmission and the existing rigidities in the labour and goods markets, would only compromise the maintenance of price stability. Instead, by maintaining price stability over the medium term, the single monetary policy makes the best contribution it can to achieving sustainable non-inflationary growth and a high level of employment, thereby supporting the general economic policies in the Community, as required by the Treaty.[9]

Indeed, maintaining price stability over the medium term has beneficial effects on general economic performance – including growth, investment and employment – and it also serves the interests of social justice: in an environment of price stability, the market mechanism will allocate resources efficiently to their most productive uses; confidence in lasting price stability removes the inflation risk premium on interest rates, thereby ensuring low real interest rates, which, in turn, will foster investment, growth and employment; and price stability helps to protect the weakest members of our society, that is to say those most exposed to the costs of inflation.

In maintaining price stability over the medium term, the Eurosystem's stability-oriented monetary policy strategy aims to take advantage of recent advances in economic research on optimal monetary policy, without losing sight of a few fundamental principles which have been at the heart of monetary economics for a long time (see Issing et al., 2001 and also ECB, 2000). To this end, it comprises two pillars. First, money is accorded a prominent role, which stems from the relationship between money and prices over the medium and long term – the relevant horizon for monetary policy-making. Second, a comprehensive analysis of a wide range of other economic and financial indicators is undertaken which typically determine price developments in the short run. These two pillars, together, provide a robust framework for a broadly based assessment of the outlook for price developments, focusing both on likely future paths of consumer prices in the euro area as a whole and on the balance of risks to price stability.

The two-pillar strategy of the Eurosystem helps to organise all the available information in a manner which permits both the internal decision-making process by the Governing Council to be structured more efficiently and the resulting decisions to be more easily conveyed to the general public. The monetary policy strategy therefore constitutes an important vehicle for communicating monetary policy decisions and explaining the reasoning behind them. In this context, the clear definition of price stability is to be interpreted as an attempt to give a specific benchmark against which the Governing Council can be held accountable.

With its strong and credible commitment to maintain price stability over the medium term, the Eurosystem's monetary policy strategy also gives reassurance about future price developments and thereby provides a firm anchor for inflation expectations. This should be a factor that helps national governments to plan their medium-term budgets in line with the provisions of the Stability and Growth Pact. With regard to wage settlements, the credible commitment of monetary policy entails that wage setters can trust – indeed must trust – that low inflation will prevail over the life of the contracts they write. Sound fiscal policies, in turn, aiming for a permanent reduction in budget deficits and debt levels will be a means of strengthening the conditions for maintaining price stability. Similarly, lasting wage moderation, which takes into account the high level of unemployment and accounts for sectoral and regional productivity differentials, will also improve the outlook for price developments.

Given the Eurosystem's monetary policy strategy, there should be no ambiguity about how the single monetary policy will respond to developments in fiscal and wage policies to the extent that they will affect the maintenance of price stability. As a result, national governments and wage setters alike should be able to design and implement the policies under their responsibility in a manner that allows for the interdependencies of these policies with the single monetary policy. Obviously, if they take the single monetary policy's credible commitment to maintain price stability as given, this will help to align expectations and condition their behaviour in a way which will lead to implicitly co-ordinated policy outcomes, while at the same time limiting policy conflicts and overall economic uncertainty.

The ECB – as a guardian of stability in a broad sense – continuously raises the awareness and the mutual understanding of the respective roles and the interdependencies of the different policies. In its Monthly Bulletin, for instance, the ECB recurrently calls for modest wage settlements – either by means of moral suasion or, if necessary, by admonition. Similarly, the ECB regularly reminds national governments to reach the medium-term commitments they made within the framework of the Stability and Growth Pact. Wage setters and national governments, in turn, are reassured that monetary policy will respond favourably to appropriate wage and fiscal policies which allow to maintain price stability over the medium term.

In this context it is important to recall that monetary policy can deliver price stability only over the medium term. This, *inter alia*, reflects the existence of some types of economic shocks which monetary policy cannot control without inducing excessively high variability in real activity and interest rates. As a result it is not always possible to keep inflation consistent with the definition of price stability. In such cases, when previously formed expectations of stable prices cannot be met, it is important for monetary policy to identify the nature of these shocks and explain their consequences to the general public.

For example, monetary policy cannot control the direct effects of oil price increases. By contrast, it is imperative for monetary policy to contain any possible second-round effects. To this end, it is important to clearly communicate that oil price increases, via their adverse impact on the costs of production, cause the terms of trade to deteriorate and thus have a negative effect on real disposable income. This loss of real income cannot be avoided for the economy as a whole. Rather, any attempts to shift the burden of this loss within the economy will endanger the continuation of non-inflationary growth. Consequently, calls for wage compensation in response to oil price increases would be highly detrimental to growth and employment prospects, since monetary policy would need to react to the resulting upward pressure on prices. Governments have to play a role in this context, namely not to convey the false impression that the costs stemming from a surge in oil prices could be avoided by relaxing budgetary policies. Such policies would ultimately undermine the prospects for long-term growth and compromise the maintenance of price stability.

The role of structural reforms

Most will agree that Europe is hampered by a number of structural impediments, which are highly detrimental to employment, investment and growth. Structural rigidities in the labour markets, for instance, and misguided incentives provided by the national social security and welfare systems are considered the major causes of the unacceptably high level of unemployment in Europe. Similarly, a high tax burden and excessive regulations in the goods markets constitute severe obstacles to investment and growth.

Obviously, macro-economic policies cannot be used to mitigate the structural causes of the relatively modest growth rates and the high levels of unemployment which weigh heavily on most European countries. Other policies, aimed at the micro level, have the necessary instruments to do so and are, therefore, responsible for ensuring durably higher growth and more favourable employment prospects. As a matter of fact, these micro policies will also help to improve the resilience of the economy to adverse shocks and thereby mitigate economic fluctuations.

As regards taxation, for instance, most European countries have expressed concern about the sustainability of the excessively high tax rates. They are currently implementing or planning reforms which will imply a significant reduction of personal income taxes and social security contributions, but also corporate income taxes. While these reforms are the outcome of an ongoing market driven process, there are views that lack of co-ordinated tax harmonisation might lead to harmful or discriminatory competition among countries trying to attract the most mobile factors of production, in particular capital. The case for tax harmonisation in Europe, however, seems not compelling on economic grounds, not least because too high levels of tax rates would stimulate capital outflows from the euro area given the increasingly globalised markets. Moreover, although initiatives to fight harmful or discriminatory tax practices are important, most observers will agree that improved tax administration and reduced complexity of tax systems rank higher in order to improve their efficient functioning. Hence, the need for broad tax harmonisation in Europe is not compelling.

Rather, among the required policies, structural reforms in the labour and goods markets must be undertaken as the key element of a comprehensive strategy for improving employment, investment and growth prospects in Europe. In this context, the conclusions of the Lisbon European Council meeting in March 2000 are highly welcome as they expand further on this issue by examining the objectives of the existing reform process and the instruments aimed at strengthening the performance of the European economy. Given the existing reform process, however, emphasis must now be placed on its effective application. Moreover, although a common understanding of the required elements is important – as well as their mutual reinforcement – the responsibility for their implementation should remain mainly with the national policy-makers and their available instruments.

While deregulation has been undertaken in some sectors, such as telecommunications, improving competitiveness is considered a prerequisite for promoting efficiency and stimulating innovations in new technologies, such as information, communication and media. To this end, as was forcefully emphasised by the Lisbon Presidency Conclusion, a shift to a knowledge-based economy would be a powerful engine for sustained growth. In this case, and given that the creation of an information and knowledge-based economy lies behind the extraordinary and favourable combination of low unemployment and subdued inflation that prevailed in the United States over the last decade, one may suspect that Europe's economy has the potential to achieve the same kind of performance as seen in the United States. Indeed, by adopting the new technologies which have been developed and tested in the United States, this may happen even more rapidly than was the case in the United States. Such an optimistic assessment of Europe's growth potential, however, seems warranted only if the required structural reforms in the goods and labour markets take place.

Alan Greenspan, for instance, has identified inflexibility in labour markets as a reason for the new technologies not having the same impact in Europe as they did in the United States (Greenspan, 2000). Further to this, he argued that 'U.S. businesses and workers appear to have benefited more from these recent developments than their counterparts in Europe or Japan. Of course, those countries have also participated in this wave of invention and innovation, but they appear to have been slower to exploit it. The relatively inflexible and, hence, more costly labour markets of these economies are a significant part of the explanation.'

Beyond the creation of more flexible labour and goods markets, there are additional factors which may justify an optimistic, forward-looking assessment of Europe's growth potential. First, globalisation continues to foster competition, which is exemplified by the restructuring of the corporate sector currently under way. Second, the completion of the Single Market facilitates the broadening and deepening of capital markets which is conducive to financial innovation and an increased provision of venture capital. The former, together with the patterns developing in portfolio allocations among European households (towards a higher share of equities and mutual funds), is particularly important for the growth of the new technological sectors of the economy, which rely heavily on equity financing. Finally, the stable policy framework in Europe itself – with a strong commitment to price stability, sound public finances and moderate wage settlements – makes a substantive contribution to favourable growth prospects.

Conclusion

The single monetary policy is credibly geared towards the maintenance of price stability over medium-term horizons as prescribed by the Maastricht

Treaty. Together with sound fiscal policies adhering to the provisions of the Stability and Growth Pact and prudent employment-oriented wage settlements which account for sectoral and regional productivity differentials, the single monetary policy can go a long way towards safeguarding favourable prospects for non-inflationary growth and increased employment in Europe.

Attempts to co-ordinate the monetary, fiscal and wage policies *ex ante* are very risky and, in the end, may destroy the balanced institutional framework in EMU with its sound and clear assignment of objectives to the individual policy-makers. All in all, such attempts are fraught with information, incentive and enforcement problems, thereby running the risk of confusing the responsibilities of the individual policy-makers. Moreover, *ex ante* co-ordination would reduce the transparency of the overall policy framework and make it more difficult for the policy-makers to be held accountable. Indeed, not least to cope with these problems, the ECB was designed as an independent institution with a clear mandate to achieve price stability.

Ultimately, ensuring sustained growth and high employment essentially depends on the adoption of a comprehensive process of structural reforms in the goods and labour markets. The time is now ripe to translate the relevant governments' intentions into deeds.

Notes

[1] Evidently, any co-ordination across different policy areas at the euro area level would first require a substantial degree of co-ordination within those policy areas which are still subject to autonomous decision-making at the individual countries level. While, in some circumstances, there may be a case for appropriate forms of cross-country co-ordination of autonomous policies, such as establishing agreements on common rules, this issue is not further addressed here.

[2] Similarly, Alesina *et al.* (2001) have recently argued that explicit co-ordination of monetary and fiscal policies may be either unnecessary or harmful: "If the monetary and fiscal authorities 'keep their houses in order' acting on their own, there is no need for explicit co-ordination. If the fiscal authorities deviate from prudent fiscal policies because of a variety of short-run political incentives and constraints, then explicit co-ordination may even be counterproductive."

[3] Surveys of the large body of literature on macro-economic policy co-ordination, focusing mainly on international dimensions, are provided by Cooper (1985) and Bryant (1995).

[4] For an account of some empirical estimates see, for instance, Currie et al. (1989). A thorough theoretical analysis that raises doubts about the effectiveness of co-ordinating national monetary policies can be found in Obstfeld and Rogoff (2000).

[5] See Frankel and Rockett (1988).

[6] A useful exposition of the role of incentives in the context of policy co-ordination can be found in Persson and Tabellini, (1995).

[7] In this context see also Winkler (1999).

[8] At the theoretical level, Dixit and Lambertini (2001), among others, have recently provided support for the fiscal policy constraints embodied in the Stability and Growth Pact. When there is a possible conflict of objectives among the monetary and fiscal authorities in a monetary union, constraints on fiscal policy, such as the debt-to-GDP limits stipulated by the Stability and Growth Pact, may be useful in shifting the fiscal reaction function and achieve more desirable policy outcomes. By contrast, if there is a clear agreement on sound and sustainable objectives among the policy authorities, this will already lead to beneficial policy outcomes without imposing such constraints. Against this background, the establishment of the Stability and Growth Pact may be seen as reflecting some scepticism about fiscal authorities' shorter-term intentions. For other studies of the effects of fiscal constraints in a monetary union see Beetsma and Uhlig (1999), Cooper and Kempf (2000) and Buti et al. (2001).

[9] A detailed discussion of this is to be found in Issing (2000),

References

Alesina, A., Galí, J., Uhlig, H., Blanchard, O. & Giavazzi, F. (2001) 'Defining a macroeconomic framework for the euro area', *Monitoring the European Central Bank*, 3, London: Centre for Economic Policy Research.

Beetsma, R. & Uhlig, H. (1999) 'An analysis of the Stability and Growth Pact, *Economic Journal*, vol. 109, pp. 546-71.

Buti, M., Roeger, W. & in't Veld, J. (2001) 'Policy conflicts and co-operation under a stability pact', *Journal of Common Market Studies*, vol. 39, no. 5, pp. 801-28.

Bryant, R. (1995)'International co-operation in the making of national economic policies: Where do we stand?', in Kenen, P. (ed.), *Understanding Interdependence: The Macroeconomics of the Open Economy*, Princeton: Princeton University Press.

Cooper, R. (1985) 'Economic interdependence and co-ordination of economic policies, in Jones, R. & Kenen, P. (eds.), *Handbook of International Economics*, vol. 2, North-Holland, Amsterdam.

Cooper R. & Kempf, H. (2000) 'Designing stabilisation policy in a monetary union', NBER Working Paper no. 7607, National Bureau of Economic Research, Cambridge, MA.

Currie, D., Holtham, G. & Hughes-Hallett, A. (1989) 'The theory and practice of international policy co-ordination: Does co-ordination pay?', in Bryant, R., Currie, D., Frenkel, J., Masson, P. & Portes R. (eds.) *Macroeconomic Policies in an Interdependent World*, Brookings Institution, Washington, DC.

Dixit, A. & Lambertini, L. (2001) 'Monetary-fiscal policy interactions and commitment versus discretion in a monetary union, *European Economic Review*, 45, pp. 977-987.

ECB (2000) 'The two pillars of the ECB's monetary policy strategy', *ECB Monthly Bulletin*, November 2000.

Frankel, J. & Rockett, K. (1988) 'International macroeconomic policy co-ordination when policy makers do not agree on the true model', *American Economic Review*, 78, 1988, pp. 318-340.

Greenspan, A. (2000) 'The evolving demand for skills', remarks at the U.S. Department of Labour National Skills Summit, Washington, D.C., April 11.

Issing, O. (2000) 'How to promote growth in the euro area: The contribution of monetary policy', *International Finance*, 3, pp. 309-327.

Issing, O., Gaspar, V., Angeloni, I. & Tristani, O. (2001) *Monetary Policy in the Euro Area: Strategy and Decision Making at the European Central Bank*, Cambridge: Cambridge University Press.

Obstfeld, M. & Rogoff, K. (2000) 'Do we really need a new international monetary compact?', NBER Working Paper No. 7864, National Bureau of Economic Research, Cambridge, MA.

Persson, T. & Tabellini, G. (1995) 'Double-edged incentives: Institutions and policy co-ordination', in G. Grossman and K. Rogoff (eds.), *Handbook of International Economics*, vol. 3, North-Holland, Amsterdam.

Winkler, B. (1999) 'Co-ordinating stability: Some remarks on the roles of monetary and fiscal policy under EMU', *Empirica*, 26, pp. 287-295.

Monetary and Fiscal Co-ordination in the Euro Area

Ray Barrell and Martin Weale

Introduction

The institutions that manage monetary and fiscal policy in Europe are unusual by the standards of other advanced economies, with responsibilities delegated to a wide range of bodies. The Union-wide institutions are largely set up by Treaty, and policy is designed to be largely guided by rules rather than by discretion. The European Central Bank (ECB) has been set the objective of maintaining price stability in the medium term, and by Treaty it is allowed to provide its own interpretation of its remit.[1] Fiscal policy is co-ordinated, or at least regulated, through the Stability and Growth Pact which imposes a ceiling on the level of borrowing except in exceptional circumstances, and also, indirectly sets target deficits. But subject to the limits imposed by the Pact, there is considerable national discretion. Nevertheless, it is not clear that due regard is paid to the interdependencies of monetary and fiscal policy, or of different national fiscal policies.

There are a number of reasons why monetary and fiscal policy in the euro area might be better co-ordinated than managed independently. Fiscal policy is believed to have some influence on local inflation rates through its effects on demand. But it is also the case that monetary policy has fiscal implications. First of all, a restrictive monetary policy is likely to depress economic activity. This will reduce tax revenues and may bring national economies closer to breaching any fiscal target. Secondly, heavily indebted economies, and particularly those whose national debt is of short maturity, are bound to find that debt interest payments rise if interest rates are high. Despite these fiscal implications of the actions of the European Central Bank, it is the national governments and not the ECB which have sole responsibility for keeping borrowing within the permitted bounds. It is not only the interaction between monetary and fiscal policies which gives rise to concern. Fiscal policies may interact. Germany's budget balance may depend on the fiscal stance adopted in France. If monetary and fiscal policies are set jointly, then it should be easier to ensure that both inflation and budgetary targets are met. If, on the other hand, policy-makers do not co-operate with each other, then each is likely to set policy taking the behaviour of the others as given. This is likely to be worse all round than the co-operative outcome.

We follow this brief introduction with a more thorough summary of recent theoretical analysis of the interactions between monetary and fiscal policy. We then proceed to an account of the institutions which make policy in the European Union and complete the paper with an empirical investigation of whether there is evidence for the use of fiscal policy for other purposes in addition to keeping budget balances at acceptable levels.

Dominance of monetary or fiscal policy

The argument above assumes that monetary and fiscal policy can be pursued effectively independently. In practice economic theory suggests some doubt about the degree of freedom available to the monetary and fiscal authorities. Sargent and Wallace (1981) argued that any attempt by delinquent fiscal authorities to offset the constraints imposed by a central bank would be unsuccessful. If the central bank maintained a restrictive monetary policy in order to control inflation, then, in the end, fiscal authorities would find government debt on an unstable trajectory. They would be forced to choose between bankruptcy and eventual fiscal restraint. Thus the monetary authority always achieves its inflation target.

In a static economy the equilibrium fiscal deficits would have to be zero. A deficit means that assets and liabilities are being accumulated, and this is inconsistent with the notion of equilibrium. But in a growing economy all that is needed is that the ratio of assets and liabilities to income is constant. The larger the ratio of national debt to national income, the larger will be the equilibrium deficit. Thus the fiscal authorities can choose between high and low debt/deficit equilibrium, subject only to the proviso that the tax rate needed to raise the interest payments needed to service the debt cannot be so high as to 1• unsustainable.[2] In the end deficit financing has to be brought under control. This argument suggests that the monetary authority will win any dispute.

More recently, an alternative view has been put forward by Woodford (1994). The fiscal theory of the price level turns the argument upside down. The argument above was that the fiscal authority eventually had to bring spending under control in order to avoid insolvency. The alternative is that the price level adjusts so as to place the fiscal authority on a stable path. A path of high deficits needs a high price level to erode the burden of existing debt. The central bank, to the extent that it sets the money stock, simply chooses the interest rate associated with this particular price level. A restrictive monetary policy will mean that a given solvent path is associated with high real interest rates. A slack monetary policy will deliver low real interest rates because it initially inflates the debt stock away. There will be some interaction, because the choice of interest rates affects the fiscal deficit, through its impact on debt service costs, and thus the price level needed to deliver solvency.

In an environment where there is only one fiscal authority, it may be unclear then, whether monetary or fiscal policy will rule the roost. But in the situation of the euro area where there are twelve fiscal authorities, it is not possible that a single area-wide price level could jump in order to restore fiscal solvency. Canzoneri, Cumby and Diba (2001) argue that, in such circumstances, some arrangement like the Stability and Growth Pact, which we discuss below, is needed to ensure that insolvent paths are avoided.

The position is perhaps, not quite as clear-cut as they make out. The monetary union does not imply a single area-wide price level. If some of the members of the monetary union adopt policies which would require price levels to jump, then that can still happen to the prices of untraded goods. Moreover, although the monetary union may lead to integration which raises the price elasticities of demand for traded goods faced by individual countries, there is no reason to believe that these will rise to infinity. Thus the fiscal theory of the price level implies that countries which adopt potentially unstable financial trajectories will see their price levels and international competitiveness adjust so as to restore solvency. Once again, countries which run potentially unsustainable deficits are likely to see their price levels rise in order to restore solvency. In aggregate the monetary authority still loses control of the price level.

This analysis appears to leave little scope or need for co-ordination, but there is still a substantial issue. The process and its dynamics are not clearly understood. The outcome is likely to be something of a muddle. In such circumstances it would be better to agree not only the targets but also the means of reaching it. We argue that the institutional framework, with its combination of inflation control and fiscal targeting has met only the first part of this requirement.

Co-ordination and the current institutional framework

The problems of co-ordination in Europe are clearly a magnitude larger than in a unitary state, as there we only have to consider a 'game' between the central bank and a single fiscal authority. In the euro area there are currently 12 country fiscal authorities and the Commission, all of whom have to 'play' to co-ordinate. There is always the possibility that unrestricted fiscal policies could lead to a 'prisoner's dilemma' outcome where all governments borrow more than is optimal. We discuss first the operation of the European Central Bank, and then the various layers of fiscal policy-making.

The ECB has an explicit objective of ensuring medium-term price stability in the euro area. In contrast to most other central banks it has the freedom to set as well as to implement policy targets. This is a stronger degree of independence than in other euro area central banks in the past and than in North America and the UK today. Medium-term price stability has been defined by the ECB to be an annual rate of (harmonised) consumer price inflation of between 0-2 per cent per annum. Price rises of up to 2 per cent may be consistent with price stability given the expected, but difficult to measure, improvements that can be achieved in product quality.

The monetary policy strategy currently followed by the ECB has two broad pillars – a reference value for broad money growth and a broadly based assessment of the outlook for price developments. The reference value for annual monetary growth has been 4 per cent per annum since the inception of the euro. This is calculated by assuming that real GDP will grow at 2.2 per cent p.a., that prices will rise by 1 per cent p.a. and that on top of this holdings of money will rise by 1 per cent per annum.

The fiscal structure is inevitably more complicated. The Amsterdam Treaty of 1998 prohibits budget deficits of more than 3 per cent of GDP and sets out a system of penalties for countries which exceed these limits. The penalties are, however, waived for countries facing severe recessions. The Maastricht Treaty of 1991 laid down earlier fiscal conditions which countries had to meet as pre-conditions for participating in the monetary union. These included the 3 per cent deficit limit and also a requirement that the stock of government debt either should not exceed 60 per cent of GDP or that, if it did, countries should be taking active measures to reduce the stock of debt to 60 per cent of GDP. This second requirement has disappeared from the Amsterdam Treaty because it is assumed that, if deficits are limited to 3 per cent of GDP, then debt stocks will eventually converge to below 60 per cent of GDP.[3]

The Stability and Growth Pact, agreed in 1997, is an arrangement for implementing and monitoring the Amsterdam Treaty limits. It requires all the members of the euro area to adopt a medium-term objective of achieving budgets close to balance or in surplus. The pact is underpinned by an 'excessive deficit procedure' involving surveillance and possible penalties. A general government budget deficit above 3 per cent of GDP is considered excessive unless the European Commission judges it to be temporary, and likely to last for only a year, and there are special circumstances. Exemption is granted automatically if there is an annual fall in output of more than 2 per cent, an event experienced only by Finland and two non-participants – the UK and Sweden, in the last forty years. Exemption may also be granted if there is a fall in output between 0.75 and 2 per cent. A failure to take corrective action to deal with a deficit judged to be excessive will lead to the imposition of financial sanctions.[4]

The Stability and Growth Pact conditions are discussed in the context of Broad Economic Policy Guidelines that are set each year by the Commission. The latter are described by the Council of Ministers (2002), the Union's legislative body, as 'at the centre of economic policy co-ordination in the European Union.' European Commission officials advise Ecofin[5], the Economic and Financial Affairs Council of the European Union on the specification and implementation of the guidelines and on questions such as whether advice or more strongly-worded warnings should be offered to particular countries. Since the fiscal limits of the Amsterdam Treaty apply only to the members of the euro area, and not to the whole of the European Union, the Eurogroup of finance ministers of euro area countries in practice handles this aspect of Ecofin business. Ecofin is the main body for discussing national economic policies. Ecofin committees discuss monetary policy with representatives of the ECB and the national Central Banks, and this is the major forum for co-ordinating such policies. Responsibility for exchange rate policy in the euro area is divided between the European Central Bank (ECB) and the Council, even though the ECB has sole responsibility for implementing monetary policy.

The Stability and Growth Pact can be seen as a device for ensuring that fiscal polices are co-ordinated in the medium term to ensure that private sector investment is not crowded out by individual governments borrowing too much and pushing up Union wide real interest rates[6] or to avoid weakening the capacity of the European Central Bank to stabilise the price level. However, this medium term co-ordination device may reduce the effectiveness of short-term co-operation and there is no evidence that short-term fiscal co-ordination as a tool of demand management is discussed.

The belief that short-term, interventionist, macroeconomic policies were often unproductive has influenced the construction of the new institutions. In particular, the decision to eschew the existence of a powerful central fiscal authority reflects, in part, this view. However, it also reflects the need to construct compromises between individual sovereign states. If fiscal policy is needed to deal with a serious problem that affects all member states, such as a major recession, then it remains available. It would be in the interests of all to use it and the institutions described above could ensure rapid and effective reactions to problems, although they may not do so, and they are not required to act. Problems that hit individual countries should be able to be dealt with within the confines of the Stability and Growth Pact, but this may need reform and clarification so that countries do have the ability to deal quickly with their own temporary problems.[7]

There have been a number of examples recently where the Commission has felt it necessary to comment on fiscal policy both because it was worried that countries might breach the rules of the Stability and Growth Pact and in order to ensure that national fiscal policy supported the ECB's monetary policy. As an example of the first type, in early 2002 the increase in the budget deficit in Germany appeared to be a matter for concern, although a significant economic slowdown was underway. As this was a demand shock, it was not clear that the German government had intentionally breached any treaty commitments, as tax rates were not being altered and spending commitments over the medium term were not being changed. Indeed, the Stability and Growth Pact is designed to allow deficits to rise when needed.

The Commission has also seen fit to offer comments on Ireland's fiscal policy, despite the fact that the country was running surpluses, and hence was not in breach of Treaty commitments. The supply shock associated with rapid growth had caused inflation to run at 7 per cent, and this was well above the Union average. Thus, this was a situation where, despite past caution about using fiscal policy for purposes of demand management and the absence of institutions to facilitate this, it was suggested that it could be used to bring local inflation under control. It was an attempt to provide some degree of co-ordination between fiscal and monetary policy, remedying a situation where fiscal authorities were concerned only with fiscal targets. At the same time, fiscal policy was subordinated to monetary policy. Because of the limited economic importance of Ireland in the euro area as a whole, there was no suggestion that the European Central Bank's monetary policy should accommodate the particular problems of Ireland.

In the final part of this paper we explore whether there is evidence in practice that fiscal policy is set taking inflation into account. This is not, in itself evidence for policy co-ordination, but it would suggest that the worst aspects of unco-ordinated policies might be avoided.

Fiscal policy and control of inflation

In figure 1 we plot inflation rates against budget surpluses for the original countries of the euro area but excluding Luxembourg. The data are for 1999 and 2000. The chart suggests a positive relationship between inflation and structural surpluses, possibly indicating that countries with high rates of inflation may be using their fiscal policy as a means of combating inflation. The picture is obviously affected by the two largest surplus figures, which represent Ireland, but even when these are omitted there is some evidence of an association.

Figure 1: Inflation and budget surpluses in the euro area

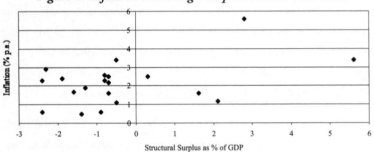

In the Appendix we present a regression analysis which explores this in more detail. We find, in particular, that, compared to other countries and after taking account of its inflation rate, Ireland's fiscal balance in 1999 and 2000 was restrictive rather than expansionary. The criticisms offered by the European Union institutions need to be seen in the light of this. But more generally, there is some evidence that countries are setting their domestic fiscal policies with reference to domestic inflation. This is desirable and should be encouraged because it helps the European Central Bank with its task.

Conclusions

The euro area has mechanisms which could be used to facilitate the co-ordination of monetary and fiscal policies and the co-ordination of fiscal policies of different member states. But there is at present no formal structure designed to ensure that this is done. The Stability and Growth Pact could helpfully be enhanced by a recognition that, where appropriate, member countries should use fiscal policy to work with the European Central Bank in managing demand and that it is the function of Ecofin to provide co-ordination of fiscal policy where practical. Such arrangements are perfectly practical provided that appropriate limits to budget deficits remain in place.

These arrangements would not weaken the independence of the European Central Bank. They might force it to be more public about its policy framework and operation, but such a change could only be welcomed.

Notes

[1] Barrell and Dury (2000) discuss the obligations and objectives of the ECB within their political framework.

[2] This is the famous 'Laffer Curve'. At a zero tax rate no tax revenue is collected. With a tax rate of 100%, the tax base will presumably shrink to zero, so that again no tax is collected. It follows that there is a maximum amount of revenue which can be collected before further tax increases lead to tax revenues turning down.

[3] With an average deficit of 3% of GDP and a growth rate of nominal GDP of 5% p.a. the debt stock would settle at 60% of GDP. In practice the growth rate is likely to be below 5% p.a., but at the same time the average deficit will be below the figure of 3% since the latter is an upper limit and not a target.

[4] These would initially have a fixed component of 0.2 per cent of GDP and a variable component reflecting the size of the excessive deficit, with a ceiling of 0.5 per cent of GDP on the total annual amount. The fines would accumulate each year until the excessive deficit is eliminated. If the deficit is corrected within two years, the fines are refunded.

[5] Ecofin in fact gains its status as representing the Council of the European Union. The latter is the European Union's legislative body and consists of one minister, acting as plenipotentiary, from each member state.

[6] Korkman (2001) discusses the SGP as a co-ordination device, and argues that its main failing is in its inability to determine an overall fiscal stance in relation to monetary and exchange rate policy. Fiscal and monetary policy can be used together to avoid misalignments, but this is difficult within SGP rules.

[7] These issues are dealt with further by Barrell and Dury (2001) and Barrell, Hurst and Pina (2002).

[8] These are calculated to exclude factors such as revenues from one-off sales of telecom's licenses.

[9] We also explored an equation linking the change in the budget surplus to the change in the inflation rate. This has only eight degrees of freedom, although with the advantage that differencing removes any country-specific effects. This gave a coefficient on the inflation rate of 0.58, but with a t-statistic of only 0.8. Thus we conclude that differencing does not materially change the coefficient, but it results in a loss of information which makes the results less well determined.

References

Barrell, R. & Dury, K. (2000) 'Choosing the Regime: Macroeconomic effects of UK entry into EMU' *Journal of Common Market Studies*, vol. 38 (4).

Barrell, R. & Dury, K. (2001) 'The Stability and Growth Pact, will it ever be breached? An analysis using stochastic simulations' in Brunila, A., Buti, M. and Franco, D. (eds.) *The Stability and Growth Pact: The Architecture of Fiscal Policy in EMU*, London: Macmillan.

Barrell, R., Hurst, A.I. & Pina, A. (2002) 'Fiscal Targets, Automatic Stabilisers and their Effects on Output' Paper presented at the Bank of Italy Workshop on Public Finance, Perugia, March 2002.

Barrell, R. & Pain, N. (2002) 'Macroeconomic management in the EU', in Brewer, T. & Boyd, G. (eds.) *Globalizing Europe*, Adelshot: Edward Elgar.

Canzoneri, M.B., Cumby, R.E. & Diba, B.T. (2001) 'Fiscal Discipline and Exchange Rate Systems', *Economic Journal*, vol. 111, pp. 667-690.

Council of Ministers (2002) 'Presidency Conclusions', Barcelona European Council 15/16th March 2002, Part III p. 3, http://ue.eu.int/en/Info/eurocouncil/index.htm.

Korkman, S. (2001) 'Fiscal Policy Co-ordination in EMU: Should it go Beyond the SGP?', in Brunila, A., Buti, M. & Franco, D. (eds.) *The Stability and Growth Pact: The Architecture of Fiscal Policy in EMU*.

Pain, N., Weale, M.R. & Young, G. (1997) 'Britain's Fiscal Problems', *Economic Journal*, vol. 107, pp. 1142-1156.

Sargent, T. & Wallace, N. (1981) 'Some Unpleasant Monetary Arithmetic' *Quarterly Review*, Federal Reserve Bank of Minneapolis, Autumn, pp. 1-17.

Woodford, M. (1994) 'Monetary Theory and Price Level Determinacy in a Cash in Advance Economy' *Economic Theory*, vol. 4, pp. 381-399.

Appendix

We use a regression analysis to explore the structural budget balances calculated by the OECD.[8] We relate these to three variables of interest. First we include the output gap, so as to explore the possibility that both revenues and expenditures are sensitive to the state of the economic cycle. Secondly, we include a role for government debt at the end of the previous year, as measured by the Maastricht criteria. A positive coefficient here would indicate that countries with large government debts are tending to run larger surpluses than those with small debts. If the treaty requirement, that those with debts above 60 per cent of GDP are making special efforts to reduce those deficits, then we should expect to see a positive coefficient. However, as we mention above, the Amsterdam Treaty may have weakened the debt stock constraint. Thirdly, we include the contemporaneous inflation rate. This assumes either that any fiscal response to inflation is prompt or that fiscal control of inflation is based on a reasonably good forecast of inflation prospects. The equation does not include factors such as proximity to general elections which may influence fiscal policy in specific countries (Pain, Weale and Young, 1997), but it should provide a means of investigating whether fiscal policy is being set at a national level to support monetary policy.

The equation is estimated for the eleven original countries of the euro area excluding Luxembourg, and using data for 1999 and 2000. The results are shown in table 1 below.

None of the parameters is statistically significant when all three variables are included in the equation. The coefficients on the output gap and on the level of government debt have the wrong signs. Removal of the output gap term does not correct the sign on the government debt term. When this variable, which remains insignificant is restricted to zero, then the resulting regression equation shows a statistically significant coefficient on the inflation term, suggesting that, on average, for every excess percentage point of inflation budget surpluses are increased by 0.7 per cent of GDP. Hence we can argue that fiscal policy might be being used to control the local inflation rate.[9]

The inflation rate for Ireland in 2000, at 5.6 per cent, was something of an outlier. All of the other inflation rates lie between 0.5 per cent p.a. and 3.4 per cent p.a. We therefore estimated the equation again excluding Ireland from the sample, and the results of this are also shown in table, 1. As can be seen, the impact on the coefficient is not material, although the t-statistic is substantially reduced. Thus the magnitude of the inflation effect on government surpluses is robust to the exclusion of Ireland. More pertinently, the mean value of the budget surplus was – 0.3 per cent of GDP and the mean inflation rate was 2.1 per cent of GPD. Ireland, with an inflation rate of 5.6 per cent p.a. should, according to the equation, have set a budget surplus of 2.2 per cent of GDP and it actually ran a surplus in 2000 of 2.8 per cent of GDP. Thus its fiscal position was more restrictive than average given its inflation rate. The criticisms of the European Commission need to be seen in this light, as fiscal policy was already being set to reduce inflationary pressures.

Table 1: Regression analysis of structural budget balances

	Output Gap (% of GDP)	Government Debt (% of GDP, start of year)	Inflation (% p.a.)	Constant	R²	S.E
Coefficient	-0.066	-0.016	0.732	-0.728	0.22	1.91
St. Dev	0.341	0.020	0.469	1.694		
t-statistic	(.19)	(.79)	(1.56)	(.43)		
Coefficient		-0.014	0.677	-0.772	0.22	1.86
St. Dev		0.018	0.365	1.631		
t-statistic		-(.81)	(1.85)	-(.47)		
Coefficient			0.727	-1.884	0.19	1.84
St. Dev			0.357	0.869		
t-statistic			(2.04)	-(2.17)		
Coefficient	excluding Ireland		0.630	-1.856	0.09	1.84
St. Dev			0.496	1.075		
t-statistic			(1.27)	-(1.73)		

The dependent variable is the general government structural financial balance measured as a percentage of GDP. The data cover the euro area 11 excluding Luxemburg for 1999 and 2000.

The co-ordination of monetary, fiscal and labour market policies in the Euro Area

Christopher Allsopp[*]

Introduction

With monetary union for twelve European countries now a reality, longer-term questions about how the economy will function macroeconomically have come to the fore. An important group of issues concerns the *co-ordination* of the different strands of macroeconomic policy – monetary policy, fiscal policy, labour market policies and perhaps the exchange rate as well.

An influential study by Alesina *et al* (2001) sets out a relatively sanguine view of the issues – which can serve as a standard of reference. For these authors, the task of the European Central Bank is to establish an appropriate inflation forecast target regime. The task for the twelve fiscal authorities is to 'keep their own houses in order', by meeting the objectives of the Stability and Growth Pact (SGP) for budget positions to be 'close to balance or in surplus' over the medium term. They go on to argue that if the system works in this way, co-ordination between the monetary and fiscal authorities is not only unnecessary but, in most circumstances would, for political economy reasons, be positively damaging. And, as far as fiscal policy is concerned,

* The views expressed are those of the author and do not necessarily reflect those of the Bank of England or of other members of the Monetary Policy Committee. The author would like to thank Iain Begg, Amit Kara and Ed Nelson for extremely helpful comments on an earlier draft of this Chapter. Some of the material draws on an earlier paper presented at a conference in Vienna to mark the 75th Anniversary of the Austrian Institute for Economic Research (WIFO). (Allsopp, 2002).

whilst there is a potential (strategic) co-ordination problem between the twelve, this is adequately dealt with by the co-operative agreement (in practice the SGP) that each country should keep its own fiscal house in order. It is also recognised that, given the other two, 'structural' or supply-side policies are important and that they may need to be co-ordinated.

There is much in this 'vision' that is convincing and the authors have a great deal to say about how policy and institutional practice could be improved to bring central bank procedures and fiscal policy more in line with the ideal. Nevertheless, there is a contrast between the vision and the apparent political reality of disputes over most aspects of macroeconomic policy within the euro area. Why should this be so? This chapter takes a closer look. It is argued that there are potentially serious issues about how monetary policy, fiscal policy and labour market issues interact within the euro area. Some of these are strategic – genuine co-ordination issues. Some are not, but it is equally important that they should be understood and addressed.

The chapter looks, first, at the reaction function of the ECB, then at the interaction between monetary policy and fiscal policy, taken as a decision variable for the group as a whole. The interaction between the separate fiscal authorities is explored; the monetary policy reaction function is important here too. The chapter goes on to discuss the interaction between fiscal policy and labour market adjustments in the euro area. It is the last of these that, potentially, seems to pose the most serious problems. A final section concludes.

Monetary policy

Monetary policy is now typically described in terms of the interest rate reaction function of the central bank. In the reaction function approach, two related but different aspects of monetary policy are conflated. The first is the 'nominal anchor' function of policy, which is typically brought in by the specification of an inflation or price level target. The second is some algorithmic rule or set of procedures (which may be conditional on the shocks experienced) which specifies (or summarises) the interest rate reactions which serve to bring inflation back to the target and ensure it is met in the longer run. The reaction function is thus a feedback system, the parameters of which determine how quickly inflation returns to target after some shock has caused a deviation. The parameters may be thought of, variously, as *ad hoc*, as descriptive of the behaviour of a central bank, or, more normatively, as derived from some optimisation procedure where the costs of deviations of inflation from target and (for example) of deviations of output from potential are traded off against each other[1]. The abstract concept of the reaction function is, in practice, embodied in an institution – the central bank.

If an inflation targeting regime is working well, it should mean not only that inflation is controlled, but also that growth will be near potential and that deviations of output from potential and deviations of inflation from target in the short term will be as small as possible. This 'having your cake and eating it' (Alesina *et al*, 2001) aspect of reaction function regimes, whereby targeting future inflation also leads to growth at potential and unemployment close to its equilibrium level, is a property of natural rate-type (or Phillips curve-type) models of how the economy works. If output gaps or unemployment gaps lead to movements in inflation, the feedback system of an inflation targeting regime will home in on a situation where inflation is at target and output is at potential. As the authors of the report put it, an inflation forecast targeting regime is an 'employment-friendly monetary policy'.

This immediately raises the question of whether the ECB's reaction function is of the appropriate type. With the caveat that it is still early to draw firm conclusions, the emerging general view is – whilst there are criticisms and suggestions for improvement – that it is (Alesina *et al*, 2001; Commission, 2001). Begg *et al* (2002), discussing ECB policy in 2001, also argue that the ECB can be seen as following a standard, offsetting, reaction function approach – though they criticise the delay in getting started. In Allsopp (2002), I noted that, contrary to public (and especially media) perceptions, ECB policy since 1999 appears to have been relatively activist. Thus, a common view is that ECB policy, judged by its actions, has been considerably better than its rhetoric.

But this would be only half an answer to the ECB's critics. Particularly in analysing the interaction of monetary policy with other policies, the forward-looking effects of the inflation-targeting regime are important. It is not just the reaction function that matters, but the *perception* of the reaction function by other policy makers and the general public. It is this *perception* that is supposed to condition the anticipations and expectations of private sector households and businesses not only about inflation, but also about future growth and unemployment – which, in turn, affect household and business behaviour. As a further illustration, consider the response to a fiscal tightening. In contemplating such action, the fiscal authorities need to be fully confident that, other things equal, this action will be followed by lower interest rates than otherwise. In the paradigm, this results not from some bargaining or co-ordination process, but from the straightforward mechanism that tighter fiscal policy, via its effects on demand and output, would lead to lower expected inflation and hence, via the ECB's reaction function, to lower interest rates.

Thus, it is important that the monetary policy reaction function should not only be appropriate, but that it should be seen to be so. Some aspects are transparent. For example, few doubt the ECB's anti-inflation credentials and surely almost no one would expect the ECB Council to want to generate surprise inflation to pull unemployment down below its equilibrium rate in the short term[2]. There is less confidence, it appears, about other aspects of the system, and in particular about the implication that, via the process of targeting future inflation, monetary policy will also be directed towards the goals of full employment and growth at potential.

The ECB's mandate

The mandate of the ECB is to maintain price stability and 'without prejudice' to that 'to support the general policies in the community as laid down in Article 2'. Article 2 of the Treaty, in turn, lays down what these objectives are. They include a high level of employment, substantial and non-inflationary growth, a high degree of competitiveness and convergence of economic performance. This lexographical (or hierarchical) ordering is, not surprisingly, subject to different interpretations. One is that it implies that the ECB is mandated to pursue goals of full employment and growth if inflation is under control. Another is that the goal of price stability is effectively the only objective that counts. (For discussion of the ECB's position, see Issing *et al*, 2001). As argued above, in an inflation-forecast targeting regime, and assuming the economy can be characterised in terms of a natural-rate structure, the pursuit of price stability is *also* the pursuit of growth and full employment. Thus, statements to the effect that price stability is the best way of promoting growth and employment in the medium term are, strictly speaking, true in such a framework. There is a danger, however, that undue focus on the goal of price stability might be misunderstood by a public not well informed about the intricacies of the system as a whole.

Transparency, accountability, and rhetorical style are not side issues. Anything that makes the new system less transparent and less well understood has the potential to impose genuine costs. And anything that reinforces the more positive, reaction function, message of commentators such as Alesina *et al* is to be welcomed. There are improvements that could help. I have argued elsewhere (Allsopp, 2002) that the ECB's target could be more explicit and more explicitly symmetrical; that the first, money supply, pillar serves in practice to confuse and should be further downplayed; and that the subsidiary objectives of the ECB mandate should be given more rhetorical weight.

A credible commitment to inflation control is essential. But so too is public understanding of how the system is supposed to work to promote growth and full employment. With a focus on the effect of the monetary policy regime on forward-looking economic behaviour, it is, perhaps, necessary to move beyond credibility, in the narrow sense, to the development of *trust* in the competence of the central bank in delivering a sensible and well-understood reaction function.

A particular difficulty in the euro area context is that, with high unemployment, it is hard for anyone to know exactly where the natural rate is. It is also true that nominal inertia appears high, which means that variations in demand may show up only slowly in inflation. Consequently, the speed with which a demand slowdown (e.g. one brought about by a tighter fiscal policy or a reduction in world trade) would lead to lower inflation and trigger an offsetting monetary policy reaction is uncertain. With doubts about the central bank's reaction function, or about its 'model' of the European economy, attempts to influence the ECB and to co-ordinate policy might arise, even though the real priority is to establish an appropriate, well-understood reaction function.

As noted above, Begg *et al* (2002) suggest that the ECB has acted in an offsetting way against demand shocks, and should take credit where credit is due. Arguably, the ECB needs to go further with the aim of establishing a fully predictable and appropriate reaction function, based on a shared model of the euro area economy, which is well understood by other policy makers within the euro area.

Fiscal policy

There is no doubt that European fiscal policy in the 1980s was on an unsustainable path. For the euro area as a whole, the debt to GDP ratio was about 40 per cent in 1980, and had nearly doubled by the mid-1990s. Budget deficits, again for the area as a whole, substantially exceeded 3 per cent of GDP for the whole of the 15 years 1980-1995. By common consent, something had to be done. The Maastricht fiscal convergence criteria, followed by the SGP, can be seen as a co-ordinated, if crude, response to the developing disequilibrium. In the period 1999-2001, the cyclically adjusted budget deficit for the euro area was lowered to about 1 per cent of GDP (OECD, 2001) and net and gross debt ratios were falling quite rapidly.

The change in policy in the 1990s owed much to the sticks and carrots of the Maastricht fiscal convergence criteria. But it also surely reflected (belated) recognition within countries of the need, in their own interests, for medium-term fiscal consolidation and control. Without this need, the SGP would probably have been much harder to negotiate. Further evidence that national self interest was at work is that countries which were not part of the Maastricht process, such as the United Kingdom and Canada, also adopted medium term goals for deficits and debt (Allsopp and Vines, 1998).

Fiscal policy for the area as a whole

What is needed for the area as a whole is a rule that ensures that the debt to GDP ratio for the Euro area does not explode, and converges to some sensible level. From this point of view, the SGP goes too far by imposing the same one-size-fits-all rule on each member country. This is discussed further below. It is useful to start, however, with the fiction that a single fiscal authority faces the single central bank.

A common presumption is that this could lead to a co-ordination problem if the fiscal authority put greater relative weight on output and the central bank put greater relative weight on inflation control. Arguably, this happened in the 1980s and first half of the 1990s when disinflation was achieved – but with the wrong mix of monetary and fiscal policy – and a cumulative effect through to rising debt ratios. The story is not particularly plausible, not least because most central banks were not independent. More plausible is the view that economic fashion favoured monetary policy and that the effects of fiscal policy were somewhat neglected – with the result that the fiscal disequilibrium was slow to be recognised.

With the fiscal authorities aware of the need for fiscal discipline, and with an independent monetary authority committed to the control of inflation, the fiscal authorities would take account of the reaction function and face a clear set of choices: they would know that fiscal laxity would lead to higher interest rates than otherwise (and a higher exchange rate), as well as a potentially exploding track for government debt. The fiscal authorities would not only be constrained by the monetary policy reaction function, but would be in a position to optimise the fiscal position (given the monetary reaction function) to produce the most favourable macroeconomic policy mix for the longer term. Moreover, for a single country, inflation and fiscal objectives are likely to be determined together, so conflicts are less likely to arise[3].

Fiscal policy is also important in stabilisation. As in the case of monetary policy reaction functions, where longer-term commitment has to be combined with an offsetting strategy against short-term shocks (involving 'constrained discretion'), fiscal policy too needs to combine longer-term commitment with a stabilisation role in the shorter term. The longer-term commitment here is to a sustainable debt and budgetary position. The sensible and understandable compromise is, typically, to combine longer-term fiscal targets with a policy of letting the automatic stabilisers do their work 'over the cycle'. The SGP commitment to be 'close to balance or in surplus' is increasingly interpreted as a medium-term requirement. If it works as intended, the SGP implies short-term fiscal stabilisation combined with quite rapidly declining debt ratios for the area as a whole – a major change from the 1980s and early 1990s.

For the system as a whole, the fiscal regime in operation clearly should affect the reaction function of the monetary authorities. For example, in the face of area-wide demand shocks, if the fiscal stabilisers are allowed to operate, interest rates need to move less to offset them than if the stabilisers were over-ridden (for example, because the SGP deficit limit of 3 per cent of GDP appeared otherwise likely to be breached in major countries). For supply shocks, on the other hand, the monetary authorities would need a more active interest rate policy than otherwise. And, in the longer term, it is plausible to argue that the relatively tight fiscal regime with a declining debt ratio would imply, via the central bank's reaction function, lower average real interest rates than in the 1980s, implying also a lower real exchange rate for the Euro area.

Multiple fiscal authorities

A common argument in favour of institutions such as the SGP is to prevent fiscal free riding. Perhaps reflecting experience of the 1980s, there was clearly a concern that some governments would be fiscally irresponsible. Under EMU, fiscal irresponsibility in one country would not lead to large and immediate costs for the country concerned, since the effect on the common interest rate would be attenuated – so, for the individual country, fiscal policy would be looser than otherwise. Fiscal laxity in one country would, however, impose costs on other (responsible) countries via spillover effects onto area-wide interest rates. The SGP, as a disciplinary device, would prevent this from happening. The no-bail-out clauses of the Maastricht Treaty are also intended to limit the potential for fiscal irresponsibility and adverse spillovers.

There is still a potential co-ordination problem, however, even if all countries individually want to carry out fiscal consolidation. For an individual country, outside EMU, fiscal consolidation would be combined with monetary relaxation, either because there was a single macroeconomic authority or because there was a well-functioning monetary policy reaction function. Within EMU, fiscal consolidation by a single country would not trigger monetary compensation to the same extent since the central bank is concerned with the aggregate effect of the fiscal actions of the twelve authorities. Only if all fiscal authorities consolidated together would the offsetting monetary reaction come through (Allsopp and Vines, 1998; Alesina *et al*, 2001).

There is thus a collective action problem that needs to be solved in ensuring the desirable degree of fiscal consolidation – which could be of a dilemma type or of a pure co-ordination type (Gatti and van Wijnbergen, 2002). As noted, the Maastricht convergence process and the SGP can be seen as ways of solving this potential collective action problem. The key point here is that the game between the fiscal authorities is not independent of the perceived reaction function of the monetary authorities. The practical political economy point is that if the ECB's reaction function were perceived to be wrong – in the sense of not assuring an offsetting monetary reaction to fiscal consolidation – this would not just lead to poor policies, but could also make desirable fiscal co-operation and co-ordination hard to achieve and, in the worst case, threaten the SGP.

Intercountry adjustment, the Stability and Growth Pact and labour markets

'National budgetary policies are in the front line when it comes to dealing with country specific shocks to real output.' (European Commission, 2001, p.64). The conventional view (as exemplified by Buti *et al*, 1998) is that meeting the medium-term objectives of the Pact is enabling or facilitating for the use of the automatic stabilisers – which are especially important in dealing with temporary asymmetric (or country-specific) shocks. The contrary view is that the SGP is constraining and dangerously over-rigid.

A first question is whether a fiscal rule is needed at all. And it is clear that there are situations where it is not. Suppose, for example, that each country, in its own interests, were to adopt sensible medium-term objectives for deficits and debts. If all countries did this and acted accordingly, debt ratios would be controlled for the group as a whole: no explicit pact would be necessary. Moreover, each country could allow its automatic stabilisers to operate, or, indeed, could use discretionary fiscal policy to improve national economic management given the common interest rate. Fiscal policy could be left to national governments. This raises specific questions about the rationale for the SGP. What is it about the common currency, and the way in which the monetary arrangements work in the Euro area, that justifies an arrangement which is as constraining as the SGP? What, in particular, are the incentives facing individual countries that could lead to problems, and what are the spillovers that could justify collective action? And what are the potential costs of the Pact itself?

In what follows, I take it for granted that that rules are needed to prevent egregiously irresponsible fiscal behaviour, so as to focus on the more ordinary incentives and spillovers that arise when the system is functioning reasonably well. I consider in turn the response to temporary, reversible 'shocks'; and then the tricky and relatively neglected issue of medium-term inter-country (or inter-regional) adjustment – which can be thought of in terms of the response to longer term or permanent 'shocks'. Temporary, reversible shocks raise issues about stabilisation. Longer-term or permanent shocks raise issues about adjustment.

The automatic stabilisers and temporary shocks

As noted, the fiscal stabilisers are helpful in offsetting country-specific or area-wide temporary domestic demand shocks. This appears to be common ground. A typical justification for the constraining medium-term objectives of the SGP is that offsets are more likely, for political-economy reasons, in the downswing than in the upswing – a tendency, which, if not checked, could lead to rising debt levels over time, and, possibly, a return to the unstable fiscal trends of the 1980s. A country-specific (temporary) adverse supply shock – which would appear as excess demand and inflationary pressure – could also be offset by fiscal action, though here the automatic stabilisers would be unhelpful. Optimal control would suggest using discretionary fiscal offsets for *temporary* supply and demand shocks if they could be reliably identified. Longer-term adverse supply shocks would require a fiscal tightening to meet the medium-term deficit objective – see below.

It should be clear that even the operation of the automatic stabilisers could pose quite difficult economic challenges in the face of some contingencies, such as a common, adverse, temporary demand shock, as happened in 2001. It could be offset by the common monetary policy, or by co-ordinated fiscal action – or by some combination, such as allowing the fiscal stabilisers to operate with the monetary authorities taking this into account. There are two obvious difficulties. One is that countries will probably disagree on the desirable combination of policies. Depending on circumstances and policy preferences, some would prefer more monetary offset, others less. Second, suppose some countries are constrained by the SGP. Those countries would prefer the monetary part of the offset to be as large as possible. Fiscal offsets elsewhere – even those arising from the operation of the automatic stabilisers – impose a negative externality, via the central bank's reaction function, on the constrained countries. The constrained countries would be better off if other countries were constrained as well.

The difficulty is that even apparently innocuous rules, such as that the automatic stabilisers should be allowed to operate, may cause political-economy difficulties unless the system as a whole is in equilibrium. This takes us to the problems of medium-term adjustment.

Medium term inter-country and inter-regional adjustment

I have noted that Alesina *et al* (2001) suggest that the task of the fiscal authorities is to keep their houses in order. The medium-term SGP requirement of zero budget balance seems innocuous – especially as monetary policy would be expected to compensate for the fiscal rule for the area as a whole. It is also notable that in mature currency areas such as the US, balanced-budget rules for second-tier (state) governments are not uncommon. Further examination suggests however, that in the European context, things may not be so simple.

In a monetary union, the savings/investment balance for the union as a whole can be brought about by adjustment of the common interest rate. For individual countries, facing the *common* interest rate, this mechanism is not available. Instead, macroeconomic balance has to be brought about by a combination of adjustment of the external balance of payments (current account), matching the divergences, country by country, between domestic private sector savings and investment, and appropriate variations in the real exchange rate – that is, by variations in the wage level in relation to productivity.

These economic implications of adopting similar fiscal objectives for the different countries of the euro area are conventional, but the ramifications are not always appreciated. They come down to the familiar prescription of 'wage flexibility', here *between countries*, with the added (macroeconomic) rider that endogenous movements in balance of payments surpluses or deficits are very much part of the process. In practice, this means that the burden of inter-country adjustment is put on relative-competitiveness changes – especially changes in relative wage levels – which need to occur so that each individual country is in macroeconomic balance and can grow at its potential rate. Overheating countries need to adjust via higher nominal wages, while countries that experience sluggish domestic demand trends and have incipient difficulties in meeting the objectives of the SGP need to react by lowering their wage costs or by improving productivity.

These adjustments, which amount to revaluations or devaluations (with appropriate changes in external balance of payments positions), but without the help of the exchange rate, may not be easy to achieve, and may pose political difficulties both for overheating and for under-competitive countries. By contrast, a more flexible or differentiated fiscal framework would mitigate some of the need – at least over the medium term – for supply-side adjustments, including changes in relative wage levels between countries, but, perhaps at the expense of postponing needed longer term inter-country adjustments.

The asymmetric operation of the SGP

In practice, medium term inter-country adjustment under the SGP within the Euro area is likely to operate both more flexibly and more asymmetrically than the above might suggest. The flexibility arises because countries that do meet the medium-term fiscal objectives of the Pact have considerable macroeconomic freedom to manage their economies via fiscal policy. The downside is that it is the uncompetitive countries that will be constrained by the Pact and will be forced to adjust via competitiveness and balance of payments improvements.

Consider, first, a country in a favourable position – growing at potential and meeting the medium-term objectives of the Pact. Suppose that, due to favourable longer-term supply-side or demand-side changes, it moves into a position of overheating and upward pressure on inflation. The logic of the adjustments outlined above is that wage and price rises should be allowed to come through – and that macroeconomic balance at potential growth would be restored by a rise in the real exchange rate. The country, however, has the alternative, since the SGP operates asymmetrically, of tightening fiscal policy to prevent overheating. The consequence would be that the tendency for the real exchange rate to rise would be offset by the move to surplus on the budget.

For the country concerned, maintaining competitiveness by a tighter fiscal policy may well look like an attractive option. Domestic inflation is more likely to appear as a policy problem rather than part of the solution. Moreover, during the adjustment process, real interest rates would, as far as domestic residents are concerned, be low, increasing inflationary pressure and possibly leading through to price rises for fixed assets such as real estate.[4] Managing an orderly upward adjustment of the real exchange rate might be hard to achieve.

The fiscal offset is likely to look like an attractive option to other countries in the euro area as well. Overheating and inflation would be seen as raising inflationary pressure in the area as a whole, and via the central bank's reaction function, triggering a higher interest rate than otherwise. Thus political pressure is likely to be towards fiscal restraint for overheating countries.[5]

So far, the euro area system has been fortunate in that divergences have, on the whole, been on the upside – towards overheating – and the countries concerned have been relatively small. But the implication of this asymmetric fiscal flexibility is that upward adjustment of relative wage levels and competitiveness is likely to be curtailed. This in turn means that it is the uncompetitive countries which find it hard to meet the objectives of the SGP that are likely to be under pressure to do much of the adjusting if adjustment is necessary.

The difficulties facing countries that need to improve their competitiveness in the longer term are obvious. The traditional mechanism is, again, the domestic Phillips curve, involving a period of unemployment and slow growth to lower wage levels relative to other countries. With low inflation in the Euro area as a whole, a substantial change could require extremely low nominal wage rises for an extended period.[6]

How serious is this problem of asymmetry in the operation of the SGP? It is suggested here that it is potentially very serious. Both France and Germany appear to face difficulties in meeting the medium term objectives of the SGP. By contrast, neighbouring countries, such as the Netherlands and Belgium, have little difficulty in meeting the SGP, but are running substantial current account balance of payments surpluses. Focusing, for brevity, on Germany, the analysis above implies that Germany needs to lower its relative costs within the euro area, and run a balance of payments surplus. (In 2000/2001, Germany had a small external current account deficit of about 1 percent of GDP). The current account surplus needs, in equilibrium at potential growth, to be large enough to balance any excess of private domestic savings over private investment so as to be consistent with the SGP – and to achieve that, it is likely that relative costs would need to be lower.

If this is right, macroeconomic equilibrium within the euro area may, to be consistent with the SGP, require a real devaluation in the euro area's largest country together with a possibly substantial move towards balance of payments surplus. In the rhetoric, this is to be achieved by 'wage flexibility' – which, stared at in a cold light, means a period of sub-par growth and unemployment to bring about a relative decline in the German wage level.

Importantly, wage restraint in Germany might not be enough. Increasingly, wage bargaining in Europe factors in wage developments in Germany. It is easy to paint a scenario where German wage restraint leads to lower wage rises elsewhere as well, leaving relativities little changed. The resulting lower inflation in the euro area, should, hopefully, allow the central bank to lower interest rates. This would help to keep growth up, easing burdens generally, but do little to bring about longer-term adjustments in relative competitiveness.

Conclusions

The conventional triad of policy responsibilities within the euro area is that monetary policy is assigned to price stability through the institution of the ECB, fiscal policy is co-ordinated via the SGP, and supply-side and structural policies, whilst extremely important in their own right, are subject to much looser forms of co-ordination. This chapter has highlighted the interactions between these broad areas of policy. An appropriate and transparent monetary policy reaction function is important, not only in its own right, but also in terms of its effect on the other areas of policy. I have argued that some of the most difficult policy challenges concern medium-term inter-country adjustments which involve the interaction between fiscal policy and supply side changes. Although the Broad Economic Policy Guidelines (BEPGs) provide an over-arching structure for thinking about these interactions, they rely at present on soft co-ordination mechanisms and lack sanctions other than 'naming and shaming'.

The problem of inter-country adjustment within a new currency area is potentially one of the most difficult economic issues of all. With separate labour markets and relatively low factor mobility, adjustment has to be via appropriate variations in competitiveness which means variations in wage levels in relation to productivity. For countries needing to improve their relative position, supply-side improvements or lower relative wages may be difficult to achieve, and may take a considerable time.

Though the potential problems are recognised in the policy formation processes of the euro area, their interconnection with fiscal policies are often neglected. An uncompetitive country can maintain growth at potential but at the expense of a tendency to run budget deficits and at the expense of delaying needed supply-side adjustments[7].

The corollary is that is that the SGP, if the medium-term objectives of 'close to balance or surplus' are interpreted rigidly, could have the unintended consequence of throwing a large burden of inter-country adjustment onto the relatively uncompetitive countries and onto balance of payments adjustment between countries.

Overall adjustment is likely to be hindered by the asymmetric way in which the fiscal objectives of the SGP have been set up. Relatively competitive countries have considerable freedom to use fiscal tightening as an alternative to the adjustment of competitiveness (towards 'worsening'). A more symmetric interpretation of fiscal objectives would be helpful to longer-term inter-country adjustment.

Given that supply-side adjustments are likely to be slow, there is a potential timing or sequencing problem. Moreover, the counterpart adjustments in other countries within EMU also need to be accepted and co-ordinated. What this means in practice is that fiscal consolidation, supply-side improvements (and balance of payments changes of the appropriate magnitude) need to be co-ordinated in the sense of being evaluated and planned together to produce a feasible adjustment path. The BEPGs offer a starting-point, but although they have chapters that cover different facets of the supply-side, they only have the status of guidelines. Moreover, many of the relevant policy measures (notably the European Employment Strategy) are conducted by other policy actors and are not well integrated with the BEPGs. The alternative of some form of economic government for the euro area is, however, deeply problematic from a political perspective.

Asymmetries could also lead to a bias towards an excessively tight policy for the area as a whole. Meeting the medium term objectives of the SGP already implies a quite rapidly falling debt ratio for the area as a whole – which goes well beyond the requirement for fiscal sustainability. Other things being equal, tighter fiscal objectives imply lower interest rates, a lower exchange rate for the euro, and a larger balance of payments surplus for the euro area. There is no presumption that the present arrangements are optimal for the euro area or that they are appropriate in the wider context of the world as a whole. A more flexible interpretation of the SGP (in the context of co-ordination with supply-side adjustments) should ease adjustment problems within the euro area as well.

As regards monetary policy, this chapter has stressed the importance not just of an appropriate reaction function for the central bank, but also that the reaction function should be fully transparent and *perceived* to be appropriate by other policy makers and by private sector economic agents. There is a reciprocal need for fiscal and other aspects of macroeconomic policy, in as far as they affect prospects for demand and inflation in the euro area, to be understood and predictable. One of the attractions of the SGP is that, if adhered to, it appears to make fiscal policy predictable. But it is much more important, for the area as a whole, and for inter-country adjustment, that the fiscal rules should be appropriately designed and co-ordinated with needed adjustments on the supply side.

Finally, what are the implications for policy within the euro area? The 'hard' mechanism of the SGP has come under considerable strain and could come under even greater strain under some contingencies – such as a substantial rise in the euro relative to the dollar. But piecemeal relaxations of the criteria or *ad hoc* toleration of violations would undermine the overall coherence of euro area policy making. What is needed is a strategic framework for medium term inter-country adjustments involving both fiscal and supply-side changes. Fiscal criteria for the area as a whole need to ensure sustainable developments for debt ratios, but, within this, could be interpreted quite flexibly. Such a change could be effected under modified and strengthened Broad Economic Policy Guidelines. An important element within this would be the co-ordination within countries of the required fiscal and supply side adjustments, which, of course, would need to be consistent with counterpart adjustments elsewhere in the euro area.

Notes

[1] A well known reaction function is the Taylor rule – originally put forward as a description of Federal Reserve behaviour – in which short-term real interest rates respond to deviations of inflation from target and of output from potential, both with a coefficient of 0.5. In practice, central banks tend to base their decisions on forecasts of inflation. One way of interpreting the output gap term in the Taylor rule is that it proxies future inflation (since inflation depends on the output gap with a lag). For a fuller discussion, see Allsopp and Vines (2000)

[2] Which would lead, in standard models, to problems of time inconsistency and an inflation bias.

[3] The UK Treasury has argued that monetary and fiscal policy are better co-ordinated with monetary policy delegated to the Bank of England than was previously the case (O'Donnell and Bhundia, 2002).

[4] This is a version of the 'Walters critique', originally applied to the Exchange Rate Mechanism, which noted that convergence of nominal interest rates would mean that high inflation countries would have low real interest rates – the opposite of what appeared to be required. I owe this point to Michael Artis.

[5] Thus, Ireland was castigated, under the Broad Economic Policy Guidelines (BEPGs) for fiscal irresponsibility despite running a large budget surplus.

[6] Some countries, notably the Netherlands, have successfully used 'social pacts' rather than unemployment to lower relative wages and improve competitiveness. In all countries, productivity increases are a preferred way of improving relative competitiveness, but policies to achieve this are hard to devise and take time.

[7] Within countries, the need for uncompetitive regions to lower wages or improve the supply side is typically offset by net fiscal transfers from the centre arising automatically from the operation of the tax and benefit system. No such process is envisaged for the euro area. In the short term and medium term, fiscal deficits can perform much the same role as fiscal transfers from the centre – though the need for longer-term adjustments remains.

References

Alesina, A., Blanchard, O., Galí, J., Giavazzi, F. & Uhlig, H. (2001) *Defining a macroeconomic framework for the Euro area,* London: Centre for Economic Policy Research.

Allsopp, C.J. (2002) 'The future of macroeconomic policy in the euro area', February, presented to the Austrian Institutute of Economic Research (WIFO), available as Discussion Paper 7, External MPC Discussion Paper Series, Bank of England (www.bankofengland.co.uk).

Allsopp, C.J. & Vines, D. (1998) 'Macroeconomic policy after EMU', *Oxford Review of Economic Policy*, 14(3), 1-23.

Allsopp, C.J. & Vines, D. (2000) 'Macroeconomic policy', *Oxford Review of Economic Policy*, 16(4), 1-32.

Begg, D., Canova, F., De Grauwe, P., Fatas, A. & Lane, P.R. *Surviving the Slowdown*, London: Centre for Economic Policy Research.

Bhundia, A. & O'Donnell, G. (2002) 'UK policy co-ordination: the importance of institutional design', *Fiscal Studies*, vol. 23, no. 1 (March), pp. 105-133.

Buti, M., Franco, D. & Ongena, H. (1998) 'Fiscal discipline and flexibility in EMU: the implementation of the Stability and Growth Pact', *Oxford Review of Economic Policy*, 14(3), 81-97.

European Commission (2001) *The EU Economy: 2001 Review, European Economy*, no. 73.

Gatti, D., and van Wijnbergen, C. (2002) 'Coordinating fiscal authorities in the Euro-zone: a key role for the ECB', *Oxford Economic Papers*, 54(1), 56-71.

Issing, O., Gaspar, V., Angeloni, I., & Tristani, O. (2001) *Monetary policy in the Euro area*, Cambridge: Cambridge University Press.

OECD (2001) *Economic Outlook*, December.

Monetary Policy is Not Enough: Pressures for Policy Change in EMU

Pier Carlo Padoan

Introduction

Early critics of EMU argued that the project had two major drawbacks, one economic and the other institutional. From the economic point of view, they argued that the euro would not meet the requirements of an optimum currency area and, therefore, that costs would exceed benefits for its members. Secondly, they argued that EMU would be plagued by an institutional disequilibrium between a supranational, unaccountable Central Bank and national governments. If these arguments were proved to be valid, EMU would probably fail.

In this paper we concentrate on the latter critique. We argue that the evolution of its economic policy machinery of EMU could eventually bring forward an efficient, viable European economic and institutional model. We discuss the relationship between the European Central Bank (ECB) and national governments by referring to the concept of policy spillover. We argue that centralisation of monetary policy in Europe leads to changes in other policy areas, such as co-ordination between the single monetary policy and national budget policies, co-ordination of national budgets, and convergence towards a 'stable budget regime' (understood as the fulfilment of the requirements of the Stability and Growth Pact). Convergence in other policy areas, such as tax policy and labour market policy may also be expected to increase over the foreseeable future.

We also argue that, over the past decades, economic policy regimes in Europe have evolved under the pressure of macroeconomic and structural integration. The transformation of the European policy regime toward a new model of EU governance holds the promise of improving policy outcomes.

Interactions between policy areas

There is some evidence that European monetary integration in general, and the introduction of the single currency in particular, are transforming the structure of the euro area towards a configuration that better reflects the requirements of an optimum currency area.[1] The evidence is mixed. In some cases, such as cyclical convergence or integrating financial markets, the evolution of EMU is pointing toward a strengthening euro area. In other cases, such as the evolution of national specialisation, words of caution are in order. Evidence on the evolution of social and labour market institutions, in addition, does not show any clear sign that a euro area model is emerging. Nonetheless, over the past two decades, under the impact of the single market and monetary integration, the EU economy has been changing in ways that facilitate adjustment in a monetary union.

An increasing convergence towards an optimal currency area configuration, however, would represent only a necessary and not a sufficient condition for a successful EMU. A convergence of national economic policies towards a coherent European model of governance is also needed. The issue of policy convergence covers two aspects. The first deals with policy spillovers (interactions), while the second deals with policy convergence strictly defined.

In the case of markets, the mechanism leading to endogenous change is deeper monetary integration. In the case of policies, the driving force is centralisation of monetary policy at a supranational level. Once the shift is made from several national monetary policies to a single, supranational policy and institution, other policy areas and institutions are affected and face pressures to adjust.

The interaction between policy areas is a more complex issue than can be fully explored here. Let us nonetheless consider the extent to which outcomes in one policy area influence outcomes in another.

Monetary and fiscal policy. Co-operation between the single monetary policy and national budget policies increases benefits in terms of improved performance. Spillovers between monetary and fiscal policy support the idea that co-ordination is beneficial. OECD (1999) simulations show that switching to a common monetary policy increases the effectiveness of monetary stabilisation to the extent that common monetary policy is geared to average and not country specific inflation rates. However, after the establishment of the ECB the exchange of information between monetary and fiscal policy authorities has become much weaker compared to, say, the EMS period, when national monetary and fiscal authorities in the ERM interacted on a permanent basis with tangible benefits for macroeconomic management. The implication is that centralisation of monetary policy requires a strengthening of the so-called 'Eurogroup' (Jacquet and Pisani Ferry 2000).

Co-operation among national fiscal policy authorities. There are other reasons to favour of a stronger Eurogroup. OECD (1999) shows that losses in the stabilisation power of budget policies decrease when the number of countries allowing automatic stabilisers to operate increases. This number, in turn, increases as budget flexibility is restored.[2] The extent to which budget co-operation in the Eurogroup increases the speed of convergence towards a 'stable budget regime' (understood as the fulfilment of the requirements of the Stability and Growth Pact) is an important issue. In a low-growth situation in the core Euroland countries (notably Germany, Italy and, partly, France) such as the one prevailing in the early days of EMU, fiscal stabilisation measures are harder to obtain. Budget co-ordination increases, if marginally, the overall growth rate, making it easier to converge to the 'stable budget regime.' Benefits from co-ordination increase if externalities can be exploited. Informal evidence suggests that these externalities are present. Within the euro area, incentives for co-ordinated policy action are larger in the core countries. At the outset of EMU, for example, peripheral countries (notably Ireland, Portugal, Spain) experienced higher growth and would have preferred a more restrictive policy stance. In this situation, the peripheral countries could tighten fiscal policy beyond the requirements of the Stability and Growth Pact while others could be somewhat more relaxed within the limits the Stability and Growth Pact.

Budget policy composition. Once financial and monetary stabilisation is obtained, attention can be shifted towards a 'qualitative approach' to budget policy focusing on the composition of expenditure and taxation. As discussed in the EC Commission document about public finances in EMU (EC Commission 2000), as financial equilibrium approaches and growth resumes in Europe, the room for tax cuts increases. However, the Commission has reiterated that tax cuts are justified only when corresponding expenditure cuts are implemented, especially in light of unfunded pension liabilities. Under this approach, new attention is given to the composition of taxation with an eye toward its implications for long term growth in particular. Once attention is shifted from aggregate revenues and expenditure to their composition, the allocation function of economic policy comes to the foreground and the interaction between the macroeconomic and the microeconomic dimensions deepens. This is becoming particularly relevant for the exploitation of the opportunities offered by information and communication technologies (ICT).[3]

Tax policy co-operation. A widely held view is that monetary union requires tax harmonisation to operate effectively under a regime of full capital mobility. An alternative view is that tax competition is beneficial as it stimulates policies to attract mobile capital and enhance the efficiency of financial markets. To the extent that tax competition produces effects on national budgets, it may interfere with co-operation among national fiscal authorities. It is not clear to what extent an 'optimal' tax regime can be designed in a monetary union. Different views and incentives are present. Core euro area countries have favoured some form of tax harmonisation. At the Feira European Council meeting in June 2000, a compromise agreement was reached under which countries will continue to set their own, different tax rates but national authorities will exchange information to prevent tax evasion. In practice, all major continental European governments (Germany, France, and Italy) have implemented, starting in 2000, major tax cuts favouring both households and business. This possibly suggests that a 'mixed regime' of tax harmonisation and competition is emerging.[4]

These linkages between monetary unification on the one hand and other economic and structural reform on the other illustrate a more general point. The launching of monetary union and the introduction of a supranational central bank lead to a growing interconnection between macro and micro (structural) policies. This makes the issue of policy convergence much more complex than generally assumed.

Policy convergence

Policy convergence in EMU is really another name for a more complex and ambitious goal: a new model of EU economic governance. In discussing this point, one has to come to terms with the unique features of EMU, the coexistence of different levels of economic sovereignty – supranational, national and local – in which the community and intergovernmental dimensions coexist.

To understand the features of the EU policy regime, it is useful to distinguish between the macro and the microeconomic domains. It is not just a question of different policy domains, however; it is rather an issue of different mechanisms and rules, i.e., different, yet interacting policy regimes. In what follows, we look at the macroeconomic (monetary-fiscal) regime and at one specific microeconomic regime, employment policies (which is dealt with at the Community level under the so-called 'Luxembourg process'), one of the few areas where some evidence of performance is available.

The stability of policy regimes is a central issue. Are regimes based on a structure of incentives that leads to mutually consistent behaviour by actors involved, both policy and market agents? Are agents' behaviours consistent with monetary union specifically? This question should be evaluated in an evolving framework. As we have argued, monetary union generates pressure for change both in markets and policies. So we have to consider whether the response of agents to the pressures arising from EMU supports monetary union itself.

The macro-economic regime

The discussion on policy interaction in the previous section leads to two conclusions. First, the creation of a supranational institution in one policy area generates pressures for change in other policy areas, in all of which at least some degree of supranationality is introduced. This suggests that a model of pure supranational monetary policy and pure national policies in other areas is unstable. Second, to the extent that a 'mixed' model of economic policy emerges, it must be based on a coherent set of incentives to produce consistent and stable outcomes. Policy convergence should be examined within this context. To discuss the point, it is useful to reconsider the evolution of macroeconomic policy regimes in place under the EMS, before EMU. This experience provided one of the main (economic) justifications for the move from the fixed exchange rate regime to a single currency, because the former was becoming increasingly unsustainable in the presence of full capital mobility.[5]

The EMS can be described as a 'weak hegemonic regime,' based on asymmetric adjustment obligations between the key country, Germany, and the periphery. The main incentive for Germany's partners was the importation of monetary discipline, and thus the exploitation of the public good of monetary stability provided by the core economy. The incentive for Germany to participate in the regime was, given domestic price stability, the support of its international competitiveness by preventing or limiting exchange rate devaluation in the periphery. The stability of the regime was obtained to the extent that national policies converged towards the German monetary policy stance. The regime collapsed when, after German unification, the core country was not willing to bear the cost of supporting the weaker (more inflation-prone) economies and the periphery was not willing to make the (deflationary) adjustment necessary to support the exchange rate regime in light of high capital mobility. The policy regime proved to be effective as an anti-inflationary mechanism, but it produced limited, if any, policy spillovers towards other areas (especially fiscal policy). The ERM crises of 1992-93 showed that policy convergence had to extend to other areas beyond monetary and exchange rate policy, if it were to pass the judgement of the markets. As long as it succeeded, it proved that an 'intergovernmental' approach to macroeconomic policy requires leadership; its failure demonstrated that weak hegemonic leadership may be insufficient when market integration deepens beyond some critical threshold.

The decision to move forward from the EMS to EMU has led to a major change in the policy regime and in the policy convergence process. Policy convergence has been witnessed with respect to both monetary and fiscal policy. More importantly, it has shifted towards a more symmetric configuration. The greater symmetry has in turn required two additional conditions in order to be effective: a) the move from a hegemonic leadership structure to a supranational one; b) the imposition of high entry costs (fulfilment of the Maastricht convergence conditions under the threat of exclusion) as well as high exit costs (the costs associated with the possibility of one country leaving the single currency). In this respect, monetary union can be described as a club good (Padoan, 1997).

The Micro-economic regime

The Stability and Growth Pact guarantees that, once monetary convergence has been obtained and a single monetary policy becomes feasible, national fiscal policies are managed according to common guidelines, including the role of automatic stabilisers. However, the sustainability of monetary union also requires progress towards the configuration of an optimum currency area. Consequently, as one cannot rely on market forces alone to produce this convergence, monetary union requires the adoption of appropriate microeconomic (structural) policies to overcome labour- and product-market rigidities. The extent of harmonisation, or convergence, of microeconomic policies towards common standards required by EMU remains to be seen and available evidence shows little recent movement in this respect.

To accelerate policy reform, the European Union has launched three sets of consultative procedures, known as the Luxembourg, Cardiff, and Cologne processes. The Cardiff process involves the adoption of measures aimed at improving the performance of product markets. The Luxembourg process deals with employment policies. The Cologne process calls for enhanced interaction between microeconomic and macroeconomic policies. The voluntary, consultative approach taken in these processes is very much still in its infancy and, in many respects, lags behind the degree of co-operation that we observe even for budget policies.

To explore the implications of this approach, consider the case of employment polices within the Luxembourg process in more detail. Because no 'institutional dumping' process seem to be at work in the EU any convergence of social policies is more likely to take the form of a 'race to the top.' It is interesting to ask, therefore, whether the existing policy framework can support such a process.

In a nutshell, the EU employment policy framework operates as follows. Each year, every EU member state sets out its National Action Plan (NAP), which contains the policy actions it has taken to improve employment. The general philosophy of the approach is that flexibility in European labour markets can be obtained by moving away from 'passive' employment policies, such as e.g. unemployment benefits, towards 'active' policies, such as welfare-to-work schemes and active learning and retraining. Within the process, however, a wide range of polices is considered, including those supporting small and medium enterprises.

Policies are implemented at the national level, as only national governments have jurisdiction over such policies, and are classified according to a (long) list of 'policy guidelines' established by the Commission. Those guidelines are grouped under four headings: employability (employment polices in the strict sense of the term, such as the creation of job placement agencies), adaptability (polices aimed at adapting workers to the new market conditions, such as retraining policies), entrepreneurship (policies aimed at improving the demand side of the labour market, such as incentives for small business), and equal opportunity (policies aimed at increasing the employment opportunities for women).

Each year, the NAP's are presented to the Commission and are reviewed by member states through a 'peer review' procedure. A final 'score' is assigned to each government, indicating the degree of fulfilment of the policy guidelines and identified 'best practices.' Policy recommendations are then directed to each member country by the Commission and the Council.

Retaining full control of policy, national governments are not subject to any explicit obligation.[6] Failure to follow recommendations brings no punishment or threat of exclusion, as was the case for the creation of the monetary union. The important point here is to note that, as we move away from policies in which the supranational element prevails or is substantial, such as monetary and fiscal policies, the intensity of the policy convergence process weakens.

Even in areas where there is no explicit obligation to adjust, however, there are substantial incentives for national governments to change policies. Two distinct sets of incentives operate: a 'competition' incentive and a 'co-operation' (regime-building) incentive. The competition incentive derives from both the policy arena and from the market. A country that performs poorly in improving its employment policies would see her reputation weaken and, consequently, her leverage in the design and implementation of EU policies at large diminish. This would be particularly worrying whenever the intergovernmental dimension is relevant. In addition, markets would punish a poor performer to the extent that inefficient policies make that country less attractive for investment, while good performers would presumably enjoy greater profitability and thus increased investment. The competition incentive will be increasingly relevant in a world of high capital mobility. In short, institutional competition will not go away; rather it may well produce a healthy improvement in EU economic performance, provided that it takes the form of exchange of best practices and provides content to the principle of subsidiarity.

The co-operation incentive is relevant to the extent that poor performance in any member of EMU weakens the performance and attractiveness of the euro area as a whole *vis-à-vis* the rest of the world. Poor policy and economic performance in any one member of the club decreases the quality of the club good (monetary union), generating a negative externality on the other club members. This should lead to a strengthened peer pressure on the poor performer from the rest of the club members (and from the Commission). In this case, the supranational pressure might be more important that the intergovernmental pressure. To the extent that such an incentive structure is strengthened, therefore, policy convergence could well be the result of the interaction of inter-governmentalism and supranationalism.

Conclusions

The theory of monetary integration shows that the benefits from monetary union increase with the degree of economic integration for a given distribution of policy preferences among countries. Given the degree of integration, convergence in the distribution of policy preferences is necessary for further benefits to be generated by monetary unification. Pre-EMU monetary convergence has led to deeper integration, thus increasing net benefits even if, at an initial stage, country policy preferences (over the inflation growth trade-off) diverged significantly. At a later stage the process of monetary integration in Europe has produced (or rather 'forced') convergence in policy preferences (towards more monetary and financial stability. However, while convergence relates to preferences for financial stability, the same is not (yet) clear for preferences and policies for more flexible product and labour markets. It remains to be seen whether the incentives to implement polices more consistent with an optimum currency area will be effective enough to produce the necessary policy adjustments. To the extent that the convergence of economic preferences and convergence of policy preferences are self-reinforcing however, EMU is indeed a self-fulfilling, evolutionary mechanism.

Finally, to the extent that EMU can be considered to be a largely endogenous process, one should ask what are the exogenous forces that are also contributing to adjustments in markets and policies that could underpin a more viable currency union?[7] A short answer is that the exogenous forces are the same ones that drive the EU integration process at large. Three main factors are particularly important.

The first factor can be understood as a regional response to the excess demand for international public goods (Padoan 2000b), which, in turn, is the consequence of the collapse of the post-war hegemonic system. Regional agreements have been strengthened as a response to external threats. As Henning (1997) suggests, whenever the US has behaved 'aggressively' in its macroeconomic and monetary relations with Europe, European countries have increased the degree of monetary co-operation among themselves in order to stem such 'aggressiveness.' Periods of 'benign' attitudes on the part of the American authorities saw a retardation or even backsliding in European monetary integration.

Henning's interpretation can be adapted to the EMU phase, which represents the highest degree of European monetary co-operation, and broadened. An 'aggressive' US attitude towards Europe would favour a European attitude of 'non-co-operation' *vis à vis* the US, and perhaps even foster an attempt to redirect abroad factors of instability inside the EU. Conversely, a benign American attitude would favour adoption of a similar attitude by Europe. Such a pattern of response would constitute 'tit-for-tat' behaviour, which, could lead to more co-operation by raising the costs of defection.

The second exogenous factor is related to the traditional European strategy of deepening integration to support its overall performance and to close the competitiveness gap with the United States. The most notable examples are the launching of then Single Market as a response to 'eurosclerosis' and the 'Lisbon strategy,' established at the Lisbon European Council in 2000 to make Europe the 'best knowledge-based economy in the world.'

The institutional response to the enlargement of the European Union to, perhaps, 27 members represents the third exogenous factor. The Nice Intergovernmental Conference has delivered a clear message. The way forward for EU integration is 'reinforced co-operation,' i.e., through initiatives taken by a subset of members, a restricted club, to move further on towards deeper integration. EMU will most likely be the most relevant example of this new institutional model and, to the extent that EMU membership increases, it would both signal the success of monetary union and represent a major engine for deeper European integration in areas beyond economic and monetary union.

Notes

[1] See Padoan (2000a) for a review of the evidence

[2] On the implications of co-operation for economic policy in EMU see Buti and Sapir (1998).

[3] Exploiting such technology requires more efficient and flexible product markets as well as more investment and integration in innovation activities. Success in these tasks can be expected to reduce unemployment accordingly. This is the focus of the so-called 'Cardiff Process.'

[4] It has been argued that tax competition has led to excessive labour tax loads, which in turn may explain a large part of European unemployment (Daveri and Tabellini 1997). So it may be that tax competition, to the extent that it leads to excessively low taxation on capital, may lead to more labour-market competition and thus adjustment.

[5] Eichengreen (1994) argues that, once full financial integration is achieved, only two monetary regimes are sustainable, monetary union or fully flexible exchange rates. Intermediate regimes such as pegged exchange rates come under heavy pressure and are likely to eventually collapse. .

[6] In some areas, of course, national governments must fulfill obligations emanating from Commission Directives such as those related to the prohibition of implementing state aids.

[7] I thank Randy Henning for raising this issue.

References

Buti, M. & Sapir, A. eds. (1998) *Economic Policy in EMU. A Study by the European Commission Services*, Oxford: Oxford University Press.

Daveri, C., Tabellini, G. (1997) *Unemployment, Growth, and Taxation in Industrial Countries*, CEPR Discussion Paper no. 1615.

Eichengreen, B. (1994) *International Monetary Arrangements for the 21ˢᵗ Century*, Washington D.C.: Brookings.

European Commission (2000) *Public Finances in EMU*, May.

Henning, R. (1997) 'Systemic Conflict and Regional Monetary Integration: The Case of Europe', *International Organization* 52 (Summer), pp. 537-74.

Jacquet, P. & Pisani-Ferry, J. (2000) 'La coordination des politiques economiques dans la zone euro: bilan et propositions, in Conseil d'Analyse Economique', *Questions Européenes*, Paris: La Documentation Francaise.

OECD (1999) *EMU. Facts, Challenges and Policies*, Paris.

Padoan, P.C. (1997) 'Regional Agreements as Clubs, the European Case', in Mansfield, E. & Milner, H. (eds.) *The Political Economy of Regionalism*, New York: Columbia University Press.

Padoan, P.C., ed. (2000a) *Employment and Growth in European Monetary Union*, Cheltenham: Edgar Elgar.

Padoan, P.C. (2000b) 'Globalization, Regionalism, and the Nation State. Top down and bottom up', in Franzini, M. & Pizzuti, R. (eds.) *Globalization, Institutions, and Social Cohesion*, Berlin and Heidelberg: Springer.

Is Euro Area Economic Policy Co-ordinated Enough?

Christopher Huhne

Policy co-ordination has become the new buzzword in the euro area, and that is precisely the problem. If more policy co-ordination is just asking for an endorsement of all good things, including motherhood and apple pie, how could anyone object? Indeed, how could anyone be in favour of unco-ordinated policy? But it is precisely the failure to define terms that can be dangerous. After all, the existing structure of economic policy – the Maastricht provisions for monetary policy conducted independently by the European Central Bank, the Stability and Growth Pact governing fiscal policy, and the Lisbon process for structural reform – is still breathtakingly new by anybody's standards. At just a little more than three years old, it is a policy-making toddler. To kill it off to try something else amounts to infanticide. The best option is to let the system work, bedding itself in, with only incremental changes as the euro area learns by doing. This is particularly the case since many of the criticisms levelled at the euro area economic framework are wide of the mark. This essay looks at the criticisms of euro area monetary and fiscal policy in turn, and examines in what sense there might be a problem, and how any incremental changes might help to resolve the issues. It also briefly looks at the co-ordination issues in structural policy.

Monetary policy and its transparency

Part of the 'policy co-ordination' sub-text is that somehow the European Central Bank has not moved quickly enough and has been too beholden to tired and out of date orthodoxies. In the Anglo-Saxon world, and particularly the financial markets, evidence for this proposition is given as the slowness to change interest rates, and the continued obeisance to monetary reference values as the first of the two monetary pillars of the ECB. For most people in the markets, these monetary reference values amount to no more than mumbo-jumbo since any stable relationship between money supply and nominal gross domestic product has long ago broken down. And without a stable velocity of circulation, money supply reference values are not much use. The critics also argue that the ECB's target range of 0-2 per cent for inflation (the rate that the ECB has defined as its Treaty objective of price stability) is insufficiently clear, and may involve a bias towards deflation.

In reality, this line of criticism begins to crumble on any close examination. There is no serious defence for monetary reference values, as there is scant basis in evidence for them. But there is a desire in Germany to continue to worship at the altar of family gods inherited from the Bundesbank. It is Germany after all which has made the greatest sacrifice of all the euro area member states as it had the most stable and popular currency. It would be more worrying if there were any sign of the ECB taking monetary reference values more seriously than did the Bundesbank, but both organisations have talked the talk without walking the walk. In both cases, monetary reference values have been honoured more in the breach than in the observance. In the case of the ECB and the Bundesbank, interest rates have been cut despite substantial overshooting of the monetary reference values.

The operational pillar seems clearly to be the second pillar, encompassing all other factors determining the inflation outlook. Here my own sympathies again are with those who would prefer the ECB to define price stability as a specific point target – say, 1 per cent in the middle of the 0-2 per cent inflation range currently set – so that overshooting or undershooting could become clear. It certainly seems likely that any attempt to steer inflation in the lower half of the range would in fact amount to price deflation, since there is under-recording of quality improvements in price indices, and the official price indices are therefore over-recording price rises, and under-recording real increases in activity. But this again scarcely seems worth going to the stake about: Jean Pisani-Ferry in various writings has suggested raising the definition of price stability from 0 to 2 per cent, to 1 to 3 per cent.[1] My own preference would also be to raise the target slightly, and to centre it on 2 per cent. But this is up to the Governing Council, and is hardly the most significant point.

What would be quite wrong would be to ask the finance ministers to set the inflation target for the ECB. This much more radical proposal, advocated by some British officials, would require a treaty change that substantially constrained the independence of the ECB. It would be wrong because it would reduce the economic and financial credibility – and in extreme circumstances the sustainability – of the Eurosystem. Although the ECB Governing Council would still have operational control over interest rates in order to meet the inflation target – as is the case with the Bank of England Monetary Policy Committee – ministers would decide from year to year what the inflation target should be. The problem with this proposal is readily appreciated from recent monetary history.

Imagine the circumstances of a serious external inflation shock: ministers would soon come under pressure to raise the inflation target to allow a more gradual adjustment back to price stability. Even if they resisted this pressure, the markets would certainly require a risk premium on fixed interest assets like government bonds to compensate for the risk that ministers might sanction a higher inflation rate, even temporarily. The result would be higher real interest rates – interest rates after allowing for inflation – and a greater deflationary impact than would otherwise occur. Such a system would be counter-productive. And that of course would be the best case: the worst case would be that ministers would substantially relax the inflation target to allow lower interest rates. The euro area could have higher inflation, higher real interest rates, and a lower path for output and employment.

In case anyone thinks that this is far-fetched, remember that there would be very little difference between such a politically-set inflation target (with implications for interest rates) and a direct political control of interest rates of the sort that British Chancellors of the Exchequer exercised until 1997. The most pertinent example of how this structure can go wrong comes from the seventies. No-one looking at the relative experience of Britain (with politically set interest rates) and Germany (with the independent Bundesbank) during that shock-strewn decade could seriously doubt the advantages of central bank independence. British inflation reached 26.9 per cent in August 1975, dipped and then peaked again at 21.9 per cent in May 1980. German inflation never went above the 8 per cent year on year rate recorded in September 1974. Yet British output growth was more volatile than German output growth, and there was no net advantage to the UK economy in jobs or unemployment. Politically-set inflation targets are merely politically-set interest rates at one remove, and the present fully independent Eurosystem, aiming at the Treaty-enshrined objective of price stability, is a clear improvement.

Nor, so far, is there any evidence that the ECB has proved excessively orthodox, or unduly restrictive in its monetary policy, which tend to be the underlying themes of these proposals. In reality, ECB interest rates have been lower in real terms than those in the UK for most of the period since the launch of the system at the beginning of 1999, despite on average higher output growth and employment growth in the euro area. The ECB has also cut interest rates on several occasions even though inflation was more than its own 0-2 per cent target range at the time, hardly the action of an inflation-obsessed central bank. Finally, there has been academic work which has succeeded in modelling the interest rate decisions of the ECB according to a Taylor rule (effectively therefore as a function of the gap between actual and potential output).[2] No such work would have been successful if the decisions were not a rational response to observed data. The ECB Governing Council can therefore be acquitted of the charge of excessive orthodoxy.

Many of the less honourable motives for 'policy co-ordination' therefore fall away, and the ECB is quite right to insist on its own unfettered right to set interest rates according to its mandate. It is particularly anxious not to indulge in *ex ante* co-ordination under which it would somehow be involved in discussions leading to a bargain: we cut interest rates in exchange for your restraint on public spending or tax cuts. If the ECB were to become involved in any such horse-trading, its independence would be fatally compromised in the eyes of the financial markets. However, it is perfectly reasonable of both the markets and the Council of Ministers to want to be able to understand how the ECB is likely to react to particular events, which might include fiscal restraint. This is where the ECB's critics are right. The ECB is not yet easy to understand or predictable in its actions.

The reason is that the ECB is still far from being the transparent and open central bank that it claims to be. It is therefore difficult for its counterparts – whether in the policy-making world or in the markets – to read its runes. True, it has made strides towards greater openness. The European Parliament's (EP's) first report on the European Central Bank (ECB) in 1999 asked for five transparency measures which would help the EP to fulfil its democratic mandate of holding the ECB to account, and would also improve communications with the markets.[3] The ECB now publishes six monthly projections, which are the forecasts that the EP asked for. It also publishes details of its econometric models. There is a good and co-operative relationship between the Economic and Monetary Affairs Committee of the EP and the ECB. In the last full reporting year, there were no fewer than 19 appearances before the committee of the six members of the Executive Board, including the four formal quarterly testimonies of the President. This is rather more, for example, than the number of appearances of Monetary Policy Committee members before the Treasury Select Committee of the House of Commons.

The ECB is, though, still short of full transparency or predictability, as was clear from the market reaction to its interest rate change in May 2001. It does not publish a summary minute of the arguments for and against, or a European equivalent of the US Fed's beige book reporting on conditions in different parts of the union. Following the May incident, the EP added a sixth transparency request, namely that the ECB should publish the balance of votes taken on monetary actions. This would require two changes: first, that the Governing Council should begin to take decisions through formal voting, which it does not do, instead of trying to reach a consensus. By operating by majority, this should accelerate the Governing Council's reaction time. And secondly that this vote should be published (although the parliament does not want the individual votes published). This would give both markets and policy-makers a clear indication of the gradual shift in the collective opinion of the governing council, exactly as analysts can now dissect the movement of opinion within the Bank of England's Monetary Policy Committee or the Swedish Riksbank. Indeed, the ECB is now the only major central bank not to publish an account of its voting. If it improved its transparency, it would improve its popularity and remove much of the surreptitious pressure aiming to curb its independence.

The conduct of fiscal policy

Turning to fiscal policy within the Eurosystem, there are again critics of the current arrangements who argue for greater co-ordination. There are arguably three levels of concern. The first simply says that economic policy is a matter to be held in common, because a loose fiscal policy in one country – particularly if a large one – may have spillover effects on other monetary union members through higher interest rates. The second says that it may be desirable to have an activist fiscal policy at least at certain times (in response to certain external shocks, or asymmetries within the monetary union). And activist fiscal policy becomes more effective if the spill-overs (of, say, a stimulative policy on neighbours' economies) are fully recognised. A third position is of those critics who believe that current arrangements are in some sense flawed because they may imply, in the crudest formulation, pro-cyclical fiscal policy (e.g. tax increases during a recession, which might make the downturn worse).

The first position is logically coherent, but the impact will not be significant if each euro area member respects its commitments under the Stability and Growth Pact, to which this essay will return. The SGP in effect provides an automatic mechanism to ensure reasonable co-ordination. On the second line of criticism, the record of activist fiscal policy does not justify the faith placed in it. In most cases, an attempt to use taxes or public spending to boost or restrain the economy operates with such long time lags that it often becomes inappropriate at the time that it takes effect. The operation of the automatic stabilisers – the Keynesian mechanism that allows the expansion of budget deficits in a recession to reflect a falling off in tax revenues or a rise in welfare spending – is the best possible policy.

True, the operation of the automatic stabilisers implicitly means that the amount of demand stabilisation depends on the level of taxation and spending (with the higher the amount, the greater the stabilisation). But it is the only type of fiscal policy that avoids serious political temptation. Politicians are always good at cutting taxes or increasing spending, but rarely at raising taxes or cutting spending. This is, after all, the main reason why it is sensible to have independent central banks in charge of monetary policy: politicians are always in favour of interest rate cuts, and rarely in favour of interest rate rises. Therefore it makes sense, in the fiscal area, to have an automatic system that does not require politicians to unwind the stimulus later, because they never seem to do so (as many European countries found during the seventies, the terrible years of lost innocence).

Moreover, a system that allowed the full use of the automatic stabilisers would be a substantial improvement on all European business cycles since the end of the Bretton Woods system of fixed but adjustable exchange rates in 1973. In each European downturn since that time, some countries were faced with having to tighten policy more than would have been warranted by their domestic circumstances, usually to forestall a vote of no-confidence from financial markets that would risk a run on the currency. This occurred whether or not the country concerned had inappropriately loose fiscal or monetary policies (e.g. the fall of the pound sterling from $2.39 in 1980 to $1.05 in 1985). Britain tightened fiscal policy in 1991 as its output fell sharply short of potential; the same occurred in the euro area in 1993. With luck, economic and monetary union has therefore provided member states with an economic environment in which they are able to use the automatic stabilisers with fewer inhibitions than was the case before.

The case of Germany, which became a cause celebre of the application of the SGP in 2002, is interesting. For critics of the SGP, Germany was being asked to tighten fiscal policy when it was least appropriate to do so, namely in the teeth of a recession. However, the story was more complicated than this. The compromise in the Eurogroup of the EU finance ministers on the embarrassing matter of Germany's budget deficit was not edifying, but it does not call for a fundamental review of the Stability and Growth Pact. Indeed, it demonstrates the need for precisely the supplementary measures that the

European Liberal Democratic and Reformist group – ELDR – has called for. The central idea is to reinforce the SGP and make its 3 per cent limit more credible.

Germany's budget deficit was projected to be 2.7 per cent of GDP in 2002, perilously close to the 3 per cent limit set in the Stability and Growth pact on which Germany itself insisted as a condition of monetary union. Yet Germany was let off without a reprimand from the Council of Ministers (despite a Commission proposal that it should be reprimanded). Was it a euro-fudge? A year before, Ireland had suffered a public reprimand from both the Commission and the Council for cutting taxes when its economy was booming. The small countries were quick to argue – Austria was voluble – that letting Germany off showed that there was one rule for the small, and another for the big. However, the two cases were different. Ireland was found to be in contravention of Broad Economic Policy Guidelines (BEPG) to which its own finance minister had somewhat rashly subscribed, namely to foreswear pro-cyclical fiscal policy.[4] By contrast, the case of Germany was more open to judgement.

The Commission claimed to be happy with the outcome of the Council's deliberations because it never sought a change in German policy. The idea was to warn Germany to meet existing plans, rather than to raise taxes or cut spending. The Commission could also point to new pledges from Hans Eichel, the German finance minister, to use any unexpected revenue to cut the deficit. Once the recovery was under way, the German government agreed that it may need to rein back spending or raise taxes. The financial markets judged this to be credible: bond yields and the exchange rate hardly changed. That is probably the right judgement. After such a pre-electoral and public wigging, the German government is unlikely to take any risks with fiscal policy. Measured by the likely outcome, the Commission's 'early warning' should be effective.

If there is a fault in the system, it is that Germany was not warned two years ago when it began to cut taxes despite its boom. Like other euro area countries, it entered the Eurosystem with a sustainable budget position, and could have happily weathered a normal recession. The Berlin government then cut taxation (particularly reforming corporation taxes) by a net 1.1 per cent of national income over the two years to 2000.[5] Without those tax cuts, its projected budget deficit in 2002 would have been a comfortable 1.6 per cent of GDP rather than scraping the limits of the SGP's 3 per cent.

Why not simply let Germany borrow more, faced as it is with a difficult economic situation? In monetary union, there has to be some limit to countries' borrowing as the markets do not on their own exercise enough discipline (look at New York City, or the repeated travails of sovereign borrowers like Argentina and Brazil). The principle of the SGP is right. Moreover, there is no inherent problem with a limit of 3 per cent even though it is a 'hard' ceiling with few let outs.[6] Recent research has shown that, providing that euro area members aim normally through the business cycle to have their budgets in surplus or close to balance, any normal recession will not push them outside the 3 per cent.[7] The German problem was caused by a relaxation of fiscal policy during the boom, rather than during the downturn.

Possible reforms

So the SGP clearly needs some more effective means of avoiding pro-cyclical policy during a boom. This is one function of the Broad Economic Policy Guidelines, but they proved ineffective in Germany's case, in part because of a view that tax cuts were good to encourage the supply-side of the German economy. The obvious solution is to reinforce the SGP and BEPG process with an agreed way of measuring budgets allowing for the business cycle. If the Council, Commission and the ECB had agreed a method of adjusting the budget for the state of the economy in each member state – as they have now done[8] – this would have provided a genuine early warning to Germany that it was cutting taxes inappropriately in the upturn. Otherwise, there is little option but to insist that countries respect the limits despite the state of their economy. Those who call for countries to be allowed to let their deficits expand in a recession, however irresponsible they may have been in the upturn, have not thought their position through. The full automatic stabilisers should be allowed to work, but only within a framework of responsible finance. There has to be some limit on nominal deficits – albeit with a safeguard on sharp recessions – if there is not to be a ratchet towards deficit finance. The

Commission should now propose, and the Council should agree, appropriate cyclically adjusted budget balances that member states should observe as an additional reinforcement to the SGP. These could be incorporated as an explicit country-by-country target in the BEPG. By maintaining discipline in the good years of upturn, they would then preserve their full flexibility to use the automatic stabilisers in any downturn.

Public investment: a key British concern

There is also, however, a separate and arguably unique British problem in current arrangements: there is now enormous political pressure to raise public investment. This was cut to 1.5 per cent of GDP in the last Conservative years between 1992-7; then it was cut again by Labour to average 0.6 per cent of GDP between 1997-2002, its lowest post-war level. No other EU country has cut public investment to such depressed levels. There is therefore little debate that UK public investment needs to rise. Normally, it is sensible to borrow to fund extra investment. That in turn runs up against the requirement of a budget position 'close to balance or in surplus' which is in both the SGP and the convergence programmes (although for 'out' countries there are no potential penalties). So the Chancellor of the Exchequer would now like extra flexibility to borrow if he is to fund the build-up without raising taxes. Without it, Britain could have to cut £10 billion from public spending (or add the same amount to taxation) to meet the deficit targets even though British public debt to GDP is low and falling.

However, the Treaty may help. Article 104 allows temporary or exceptional deficits and specifically asks the Commission to take into account whether the deficit exceeds government investment. If the Chancellor wants to join the euro – thereby making the UK liable for fines if we fail to keep within the borrowing limits – there is surely the flexibility here with the Commission to allow extra borrowing to catch up on Britain's past under-investment. Indeed, that flexibility was exercised by the Finance Ministers in February 2001 when they refused to confirm the Commission's attempt to censure the UK. The problem would then potentially be that such an enlarged deficit could make the UK more prone to breaking the 3 per cent limit in the SGP.

However, a recent study by the National Institute of Economic and Social Research calculates that Britain could run a budget deficit through the business cycle of at least 1.3 per cent of GDP without facing more than a 1 per cent risk of exceeding the 3 per cent limit.[9] The NIESR team argue that budget outturns have become less volatile because the economy is less volatile, and this consequently increases the amount that governments can safely borrow and still stay within the overall limit. In practical terms, therefore, the current fiscal arrangements are adequate not only to provide Britain with the full operation of the automatic stabilisers in a recession, but also to fund the Chancellor's desired level of public investment.

The SGP and the debt ratio

The UK case raises the broader issue; of course, of whether in the long term it makes sense to have a Stability and Growth Pact whose current provisions mean steadily declining public debt to GDP ratios. These occur regardless of the assets being acquired on the other side of the public sector balance sheet, and regardless of whether the countries concerned have substantial contingent liabilities. The SGP could imply a steadily improving net asset position for national governments, for which there is no obvious economic raison d'être. However, this is not an imminent problem, and it seems poor timing to determine a long-term change at the point when the SGP is coming under strain. Eventually, the solution to the problem may be to allow the SGP's constraints to ease somewhat for countries whose public debt to GDP ratio is clearly within responsible limits (say, below 40 per cent).

Co-ordination of structural policies

The third key area where policy co-ordination is already mandated in the EU procedures is structural policy, where the various summit processes (Cardiff, Luxembourg, Lisbon) involve peer review around benchmarked performance. Clearly, there are important spill-overs from the degree of flexibility and reform in one euro area economy to another. In extremis, a large euro area economy with a high rate of structural unemployment[10] may cause inflationary pressures to arise in the euro area at an earlier point in any upturn than would otherwise have occurred. So co-ordination makes sense. But the remedies to most of these problems are within the competence purely of national governments, so that the process of peer review is probably the only realistic way of making progress with the detailed dossiers.

It is early days to assess the success of the process, which began in earnest only with the Lisbon summit in 2000. So far, the results are mixed. There is still negligible progress on a community patent (blocked because of insistence on different languages), a single sky, and full energy liberalisation including domestic markets. The European Parliament blocked the take-over directive, which would have established common rules to protect minority investors. The Council of Ministers has so far failed to agree on common rules for the management of pension funds. On the plus side, the European Parliament has voted for a compromise with the Council of Ministers on the adoption of international accounting standards in the EU by 2005, ending years of haggling. The Parliament has also agreed to 'fast-track' financial services measures to incorporate the delegated decision-making suggested by Baron Lamfalussy's wise men.

At national level, there has been progress on labour market reform. Overall, the euro area created more jobs than the United States in the five years to 2001. However, the most convincing reform has been in the peripheral member states. The overall decline of unemployment from its peak rates in the eighties is now impressive in Spain (down by 11.3 per cent of the labour force), Finland (down 7.4 per cent), Ireland (down 12.7 per cent), and the Netherlands (down 7.8 per cent).[11] All these countries have outperformed Britain (down 6.2 per cent). Six other EU countries now have lower unemployment rates than Britain. Progress is less impressive in the three big euro area member states of Germany, France and Italy (down 1.8, 2.5 and 3.6 percentage points respectively). Italy may be changing under Silvio Berlusconi, but the appetite of either the French or the German governments for serious reform will only be tested now that their elections are concluded.

Concluding remarks

In sum, there is a role for economic policy co-ordination, but those who call for more of it tend to underestimate how much there already is. Within the Eurosystem's framework, three is an implicitly co-ordinated system. The monetary policy of the ECB is far more pragmatic than critics suggest, and is difficult to fault in retrospect. The key area where progress is still needed is transparency, as the European Parliament has correctly and repeatedly stressed. The fiscal policy framework – the Stability and Growth Pact – should in fact deliver a greater degree of fiscal stabilisation than was ever attained under the regime of free floating exchange rates, when fiscal policy often proved to be pro-cyclical. However, if it is to work it must ensure that discipline is maintained in the good years so that fiscal policy can be fully used to support activity in the bad years. To ask for more than this seems over-ambitious given the past track record of pro-cyclical attempts at fine-tuning. Compared with the world of old constraints, the EMU macro-economic policy regime looks like a distinct improvement. On structural policy, the EU is moving, albeit slowly. But the process of competition and comparison of best practice should bring dividends. Give the new regime time. With a little marginal adjustment – and much more openness – it might work surprisingly well.

Notes

[1] For example, Pascal Lamy and Jean Pisani-Ferry *The Europe we want*, Policy Network, London, 2002.

[2] See Peter Bofinger *Monetary Policy: Goals, Institutions, Strategies, and Instruments* Oxford University Press, December 2001.

[3] European Parliament resolution on the annual report for 1998 of the European Central Bank (C4-0211/1999) Rapporteur: Christopher Huhne.

[4] A separate issue is whether the Commission really understood the inflationary process in Ireland, and was therefore well advised to embark on a reprimand. In such a small, open economy the inflation rate is driven primarily by the exchange rate (particularly since Ireland does so much trade outside the euro area) and not by small changes in fiscal policy whose demand impact is principally on Ireland's trading partners.

[5] This uses the OECD measure of structural budget balances. See Annex Table 31 of the *OECD Economic Outlook*, December 2001. The German general government structural deficit moved from 0.9 per cent of GDP in 1999 to 2 per cent in 2001.

[6] Article 2 of council regulation no 1467/97 states that the Commission, when preparing a report on an excessive deficit, shall normally consider only a fall of GDP of more than 2 per cent as 'exceptional' but it immediately notes that the Council of ministers shall take into account any observations from the member state 'showing that an annual fall of real GDP of less than 2 per cent is nevertheless exceptional in the light of further supporting evidence, in particular the abruptness of the downturn or on the accumulated loss of output relative to past trends'.

[7] See for example Buti M, Franco D and Ongena H 'Budgetary policies during recessions: retrospective application of the Stability and Growth pact to the post-war period' in *Recherches Économiques de Louvain*, 63 (4), 1997 and also Ray Barrell and Karen Dury 'Will the SGP ever be breached?' in *The Stability and Growth Pact: the architecture of fiscal policy in EMU* ed. by Anne Brunila, Marco Buti and Daniele Franco, Palgrave, 2001.

[8] There is now a common methodological approach to cyclical adjustment of budget balances (evidence of DG Ecfin officials to the economic and monetary affairs committee, 27th March 2002). This is a necessary condition of making structural budget balances an operational target.

[9] Barrell and Dury op.cit.

[10] Ie Non-Accelerating Inflation Rate of Unemployment (NAIRU).

[11] These are standardised unemployment rates (ILO definition) comparing the peak annual rate in the seventies or eighties with the unemployment rate at the end of 2001, taken from HM Treasury Pocket Databank.

Is the Tail Wagging the Dog?
Formal and informal economic
policy co-ordination in EMU

Klaus Gretschmann[*]

Starting point: the contested issue of policy co-ordination for a new European economic order

The process of European integration, the driving forces of which have varied over time – initially trade-driven (customs union), then factor-driven (single market) and money-driven (EMU), and most recently innovation-driven (Lisbon process) – has not been accompanied by strong co-ordination efforts in the macro-economic realm. Whilst Article 99 of the European Treaty (in its new version since Maastricht) requires member states to consider their individual economic policies as a matter of common interest, the reality is that policy co-ordination still appears to be rather weak. It was indeed only the 'unionisation' of monetary policy through EMU that brought the issue of how much centralisation and co-ordination of public spending, taxation, income policies and structural reform is needed to the forefront of the European debate (Alesina et al 2001).

Under the impetus of EMU, 'Euroland' is effectively becoming a genuinely unified 'European Economy', characterised by a single monetary authority (the ECB) working alongside prevailing national governmental

---

[*] The views expressed here are given in a purely personal capacity of the author and do not represent the position of any institution.

bodies, which determine and dominate national macro-economic policy-making, and thereby, the overall economic situation in the EU. This institutional arrangement raises questions of policy consistency, of compatibility of decisions and instruments, as well as of the timing and extent of policy changes both between the ECB and national governments on the one hand, and between individual national budget and tax authorities on the other.

'There is no reason', Korkman (2002 : 296) argues convincingly, 'to expect that the sum of the fiscal policies of 12 individual [euro area] member states is always appropriate for the euro area'. There seems to be general agreement that a genuine European economic policy in its own right is necessary, and that it should not be modelled on a single Member State's approach – be it German, French, British, Dutch or whatever else. The problem, however, is that there is as yet no clear vision of where we are heading, nor is it evident which of the features from different national systems should be adopted.

The fact that this is still a 'desideratum' is due to the complicated and fuzzy political foundations of EMU. This chapter explores why this is the case, looks at different aspects of the co-ordination debate, notably the international dimension, and suggests options for a way forward. The next two sections discuss how national interests are served by enhanced co-ordination and the forms it might take. We then examine and offer a critique of current arrangements, stressing the roles of informal bodies and the tensions in the euro area's external representation, and conclude with some proposals.

Co-ordination and national interests

Basically, nations seek to increase their power in international monetary and economic relations in order to create conditions that minimize the costs of pursuing their domestic economic priorities in an interdependent world economy. Their policy choices are conditioned by the constraints and opportunities they face in the international environment.

Therefore, Moravcsik (1993) argues convincingly that both the demand and the willingness to integrate and co-ordinate are determined by the extent to which it is necessary to manage international interdepence. It seems to be a kind of generic law in integration that whenever a nation's ability to control its economy is constrained by either market forces – the most prominent of which is international capital mobility – or by spill-overs from economic policy measures abroad, integration provides a tool for regaining control and material sovereignty at a supra-national level, through the pooling of resources, co-operative governance, and institutionalisation of rules for policy-making.

Institutionalisation is an indispensable prerequisite for the stabilisation of future behaviour and limiting the future strategies of the various players and, in so doing, it contributes to reducing volatility and enables the players to form rational and reliable expectations about the future course of events.

The price to be paid for interdependence is a relative loss of national decision-making autonomy. Under conditions of interdependence, the ability of a government to pursue its own domestic economic priorities is constrained by external forces, over which it normally has little or no control. However, states possess different degrees of power to change the international environment within which these external forces operate. The more powerful a country and its (economic) institutions, the more easily it can externalise the costs of pursuing its domestic (economic) priorities. At the same time, however, countries wish to avoid or limit the negative consequences for them of other governments' pursuit of domestic economic priorities. This makes it clear that countries will accept provisions for co-ordination only if they afford sufficient scope for the pursuit of their own domestic goals.

Against this background it will be necessary to reconcile conflicting national preferences, perceptions, interests and 'beliefs'. This is particularly relevant since EMU did not start out with a shared, consistent and coherent concept of economic policy making for Europe as a whole, but rather was built on the introduction and management of a single currency. Its founders expected the necessary macro economic and fiscal institutions, instruments and policy content to flow from monetary policy pressure. This idea fits in with the neofunctionalist logic of integration, but neglects the power and influence of political and economic vested interests. Is the tail trying to wag the dog?

Inconclusive evidence: the lukewarm quest for co-ordination and the 'dissensus' on the right model

The quest for economic policy co-ordination raises the following questions:

- What and how much leeway should be reserved for national policy making?
- To what extent is a unified aggregate fiscal policy needed to complement monetary policy at the macro level?
- Can wage and income policies be altered by government action or do they have to be taken as an independent variable?
- Is there a single one-best policy mix identifiable for Europe and what is it like ?

The answers to these questions – both in the theoretical literature and in political circles – are inconclusive. In relation to the first two questions, one strand of thought argues that, with a centralized monetary policy that lacks differentiation according to local and regional needs, a differentiated local policy response to asymmetric conditions and unevenly distributed macro problems can only be delivered through decentralized fiscal policy instruments. In this case, co-ordination means that there remain national toolkits and co-ordinated but different policy responses. Another strand of thought is that is essential to complement the common monetary policy for the euro area with one single fiscal policy in order to make macro policy more transparent and calculable for market participants.

As regards the third and fourth questions, there seems to be a consensus among experts that the steering capacities of policies in the income domain is very limited. Therefore, it is important, as some argue, to actively co-ordinate fiscal and monetary measures at the European level. This is justified when there are strong mutual links between monetary and fiscal impulses (Kotz 1996). Others, particularly proponents of the former Bundesbank policy, believe in a strong separability of monetary and fiscal measures. They argue in favour of a clear compartmentalization of policies : wage policy should be exclusively a matter for the social partners, monetary policy is supposed to be run by the ECB on anti-inflation objectives; growth policy and anti-cyclical policies should remain in the hands of the national treasuries in the continuing absence of full synchronisation of economic cycles in Europe.

Against this background the only real consensus appears trivial: if national policy choices are irrelevant for other countries, i.e. in the case of zero externalities, co-ordination is dispensable. Should national economic policy making produce welfare gains or losses in other countries or for the Union, the case for co-ordination is compelling.

Co-ordination is particularly difficult if policy makers do not agree on the 'true model', that is an accurate characterisation of how the economy functions:

- There may be disagreement about the effects (whether in their scale or their nature) of specific policy changes on policy targets (*differences in beliefs*);
- There may be cross-country differences in the degree of (inter)dependence (*differences in spill-over effects*);
- There may be different models of how national economies and the global economy work (*model uncertainties*).

Decisions-makers usually have only limited knowledge about the functioning of their national economies. They know even less about the working of the European economy in its entirety. This means they are faced with the problem of having to decide between competing models, the properties and premises of which are only partially understood. This is already an intractable problem at national level. It will be even harder to solve and even more complicated at the international level. Feldstein (1988) and Frenkel and Rockett (1988) have proven conclusively that if policy-makers do not agree on the true model, co-ordination may well entail welfare losses. In any international setting like the EU, the probability that there is model certainty and consensus is pretty low. The more uncertain and less consensual a policy model is, the less aggressively policy-makers will use their policy instruments.

Siebert (1997) pointed out that the conduct of a joint optimal economic policy would require near-perfect agreement on the model and the philosophy on which an economic policy is to be founded. In the same vein, he argues that a coherent and jointly acceptable paradigm of economic explanation and analysis is an indispensable prerequisite. The former Belgian Minister of Finance and current President of the European Investment Bank, Philippe Maystadt, has expressed regret that member states' co-ordination efforts have been largely limited to efforts to prevent free-riding, i.e. that co-ordination has been primarily defensive in nature, and that there is unwillingness to engage forcefully in active macro-economic policy co-ordination. This suggests that divergence rather than convergence still prevails with regard to economic models, philosophies and beliefs in euro area member states.

In principle, governments can co-ordinate either through *intergovernmental arrangements* or through *a transfer of sovereignty to a common institution* (von Hagen, Mundschenk 2001). The more binding arrangement is, of course, the latter. The main problem is multi-dimensional and is confronted by the following dilemmas:

- So long as there is no consensus on economic models and measures, self-binding arrangements are difficult to achieve;
- So long as it is not clear which interests prevail in the common supra-national institution and whether it can be trusted to pursue the common goal, transfer of sovereignty is risky; and
- So long as spending and taxation are about the level and composition of *national* public goods and *at the same time* about European macro-economic policy, a sacrifice of the former for the sake of the latter – in the face of varying national preferences – is very improbable.

Therefore, loose forms of co-ordination are to be preferred and a clear majority of euro area member states seem to agree with Commissioner Solbes (2002:5) that economic policy co-ordination 'should not be seen to pursue a centralised economic governance with a uniform policy response to economic challenges, national policy should continue to have sufficient latitude to formulate and implement policies tailored to their needs.'

Present provisions: processes, guidelines, pacts under scrutiny

Economic policy co-ordination, as it is understood in the Brussels context, by no means dovetails with how it is conceived of in academic economics. In principle, economic co-ordination may have a narrow or a broad meaning (von Hagen and Mundschenk, 2001). The former implies a 'simple' surveillance and monitoring of national policies of EU member states in order to veto those national policies that are expected to produce – Paretian – welfare losses for the EU as a whole. Under this *regime-related co-ordination* come the Excessive Deficit Procedure and the Stability and Growth Pact as well as – to a somewhat lesser extent – the Broad Economic Policy Guidelines. The co-ordination task is to identify and measure policies that might affect the EU's welfare position adversely and, in response, to push member states to refrain from adopting such policies. The broader notion of *strategic policy co-ordination* aims at developing co-operative policies in order to maximise welfare gains and positive externalities from policies adopted by one country that could affect economic variables in other countries. In this sense, the aim is not harmonisation of policy, but ensuring that it evolves in a co-ordinated manner.

Even though empirical studies come to the conclusion that externalities are generally too small and insignificant to justify explicit policy co-ordination (Buti and Sapir 1998), co-ordination of economic policy-making refers to the strategic aims. However, in view of the complexities of designing and implementing co-ordinated systems of discretionary national policies, the risk of failure is high. Hence the reticence of European policy makers and officials to take up the broader view.

Against the above background, EMU constitutes an economic policy regime based on three pillars, the ECB, the Excessive Deficit Procedure and the Broad Economic Policy Guidelines (Korkman 2002:288). Within this triangle, the core instrument of policy co-ordination is the Stability and Growth Pact, the functions of which centre less on co-ordination and more on mutual surveillance and control of the budgetary policies of member states. It is primarily meant to prevent 'free-rider' behaviour by member states that might otherwise be tempted to run excessive deficits, but it leaves aside the issue of what the appropriate aggregate fiscal policy stance should be. Admittedly, there are other co-ordination efforts in the making, such as Financial Market Supervision, which becomes operational in 2005, or minimum rates in the area of energy taxation. However, in essence the opportunities for co-ordination at present are embedded in a complex structure of responsibilities, competences, consultation mechanisms and guidelines and processes.

As the Lisbon European Council emphasized, the Broad Economic Policy Guidelines are the core element of co-ordination at union level. Alongside general economic considerations and the assessment of the policy mix in Euroland, the BEPGs contain recommendations for policy measures in the area of fiscal, income and structural policies in individual member states. Although the level of commitment is relatively strong, the de-facto success of the BEPG is still dubious.

On 22 May 2002, the European Commission adopted its Communication 'A Project for the EU' in which it pleaded strongly for strengthening economic policy co-ordination. Its basic objectives were:

- Being able to attain a common assessment of the economic situation in the EU;
- To reach agreement on adequate policy responses;
- To obtain the power to implement the necessary measures;
- To have an instrument to promote growth and job creation for Europe as a whole.

This was to be achieved by – among other things – turning the BEPG from recommendations into proposals under the Treaty. Such a change would allow the Commission to be able to discipline governments without prior approval from the finance ministers by qualified majority. In effect, finance ministers would only be able to override the Commission with a unanimous vote.

Less powerful as an instrument for joint economic policy-making in Euroland are the different processes of co-ordination the EU has established. Neither the *Luxembourg Process* (since 1997) providing guidelines for employment policy and promoting 'employability', 'adaptability', entrepreneurship etc as a basis for national action plans for employment; nor the *Cardiff Process* (since 1998) dealing with the improvement of competitiveness and the efficiency of the Single Market will be able to realise their full potential unless the convergence of models and beliefs discussed above is achieved. This is particularly evident in the case of the so-called

Cologne-Process (since 1999), which contains as a core element the '*macro-economic dialogue*'. Its purpose is to integrate the views of the different political actors and social and economic partners in an informal consultation process. The Dialogue has no decision or enforcement capability. Its aim is to share relevant policy information.

The process which reflects the strongest consensus among European Governments in the field of economic policy is the *Lisbon Process* (since 2000). It contains a highly ambitious program of structural reform aimed at helping the EU to catch up with the US by 2010 at the latest, and a commitment to promote a European knowledge economy and society. Its two major procedural novelties were:

- The establishment of a regular Spring Summit of the European Council to deal with progress on the Lisbon agenda; and
- The so-called 'open method of co-ordination'.

The open method of co-ordination is a device to facilitate economic, fiscal and social policy co-ordination under conditions of economic diversity. Introduced in the Maastricht and Amsterdam Treaties, it was generalized as a generic method by the Lisbon Summit. The method suggests that member states agree to define policy objectives and problems as matters of common concern whilst the actual choice of effective policies remains a national responsibility. The outcomes of national policy-making in pursuit of the commonly defined objectives are regularly evaluated and benchmarked by peer review and public scrutiny. In so doing, the open method of co-ordination has become a key means of advancing institutional competition and co-ordination.

Informal provisions

In spite of the elements outlined above, conventional wisdom holds that policy co-ordination under EMU remains too insubstantial, not least because it relies so much on non-binding, sub-optimal instruments and a complex system of multilevel decision-making (Jacquet, Pisani-Ferry 2000). Two examples are the Eurogroup and the informal 'sherpas' and bilateral groups which help to prepare more formal meetings.

The Eurogroup

When looking for a core institution to guide the co-ordination process, it becomes evident that the group of the 12 EU member states that introduced the Euro, the informal so-called Eurogroup, has played a pivotal role in this regard. Even though the Eurogroup lacks Treaty foundation, i.e. a formal legal basis, it has contributed considerably to analysing and clarifying positions, forging consensus, evaluating options, etc. via peer review. The importance of the Eurogroup cannot be emphasized enough. This is due to the fact that the group is an informal one, that it is very small, that it meets without a large number of staffers and civil servants, that – therefore – discussions are very frank and straight forward, based on thorough policy-relevant analysis and spontaneous discussion rather than boring speaking notes read to the audience. It provides for *free exchange of information in a culture of discourse*. ECB President Duisenberg praised the Eurogroup recently by pointing out that ever since its inception he had missed only *one*(!) meeting of the Eurogroup, whereas he very often sends a deputy to Ecofin meetings.

The Eurogroup has become so successful as an informal co-ordination forum that its original purpose, to serve as a temporary device to be abolished once all EU member states have introduced the euro, has given way to the idea that it may be turned into a more formal body in the face of the enlargment process. The Commission recently (COM 2002) launched the idea of transforming the present Eurogroup into a Euro-ECOFIN Council in order to give the countries of the euro area full competence to take binding decisions. This idea had already been suggested by President Chirac of France in December 2001 under the heading of 'enhanced economic co-operation' of euro area countries in the face of enlargement. The crucial question is whether European citizens are willing and prepared to trust the informal – and therefore non-transparant – peer group processes.

Sherpas and bilateral groups

In order to circumvent heavy-handed bureaucracies and to streamline a system of incomplete but complex and complicated co-ordination, other informal institutional arrangements have also emerged.

For the preparation of European Councils, the Heads of States and Governments have appointed personal representatives. These personalities, mainly chief economists or economic advisors of the Heads themselves, active in the centres of power, have been meeting outside formal channels to co-ordinate national economic policy design at the highest levels. They have been named the Europe Sherpas, a name borrowed from the native people hired to carry the heavy loads and equipment for mountaineers in the Himalayas.

Moreover, regular informal meetings take place on a bilateral basis between the chief economists and their teams in national headquarters. Examples are the 'groupe pilotage' (French Matignon – German Chancellery), or the German-British Working Group (10 Downing Street – German Chancellery). The objectives are to share *information* (about the national economic situation and possible policy measures), *communication* (about 'externalisation' and 'impact'), *co-ordination* (to prevent undesirable side effects or to mutually reinforce virtuous effects), and *co-operation* (where it appears useful).

The results of such talks are then fed into the normal and formal decision structures at both the national and – where appropriate – the European level.

Pressing problem: how to co-ordinate the external representation of the euro area

Despite the informal though useful co-ordination arrangements outlined above, the absence of a principal political authority representing the euro area has proven to be a major obstacle for an adequate international representation in the G7 and the international financial institutions (notably IMF and World Bank). Whilst a seat has been reserved for the ECB president at the G7 table – replacing the G7 national central bank presidents when it comes to discussing exchange rates, interest rates or global economic cycles – a satisfactory and convincing arrangement for the Eurogroup President has not been found; particular problems arise in cases in which the 6 monthly Presidency is held by a non-G7 euro area country. The reason is that 4 of the G7 members are EU countries and adding the Eurogroup President would lead to an even stronger regional imbalance. Moreover, the Vienna European Council of December 1998 agreed that a representative of the Commission should also be a member of the EU delegation at G7 meetings. In the face of fierce resistance by the US, the Europeans did not make use of this provision.

As regards the issue of external representation, the Commission (2002) has made a strong case for streamlining and strengthening the external representation of the euro area in international financial organisations by giving this assignment to a Commissioner responsible for economic and financial policy. However, this touches upon the particularly sensitive point of national power and prestige in international fiscal and financial diplomacy.

Present arrangements have few supporters, as they are suited to a fragmented economic Europe, not an integrated one. As regards the role of the ECB vis-a-vis the national central banks, it is not too far-fetched to assume that, over time, the President of the ECB will fully replace the national bank presidents of Germany, Italy, France and, assuming the country adopts the euro, the UK in G7 meetings.

But the EU also badly needs a prominent figure operating alongside the President of the ECB, a *European Foreign Finance Minister*. But who should best take on this role? In principle, three options can be envisaged:

- The Commissioner responsible for Economics and Finance;
- The President of the ECOFIN or euro-group;
- A Deputy General-Secretary or, if created, a Vice-President of the Council.

Since – in the present institutional framework – no Commissioner, however brilliant, can summon the necessary strength and political legitimacy to be a strong counterpart to the US Treasury Secretary while national competences in economic policy making remain, the first option lacks conviction. Nor is the second model very compelling: the system of rotating 6-monthly presidencies cannot provide continuity and will not be accepted by Europe's international partners. What remains is the third option, even though it, too, encounters stiff resistance from a political point of view.

A compromise solution may lie in a radical reform of the presidency system, as advocated recently by some member state governments. The rotating presidency would be replaced by a single individual who would hold the job of 'European President' for 5 years. This President would report directly to the national leaders. In order to get the necessary approval from all member states for such a model – which could upset the delicate balance in the power structure between Council, Commission and Parliament in favour of the first of these institutions – a system of up to 3 Vice Presidents could share responsibilities with the President. Each of these Vice Presidents, whose nominations might reflect the North-South, East-West and Big-Small interest cleavages, would need to be given a substantive portfolio. In this design, the first Vice President could very well take over the role of a *Foreign Finance Minister* of the Union. The same type of model could be followed if, as is at present, there is not a President, but a General-Secretary and High Representative though in a new longer term group presidency arrangement. In this case the group holding the presidency could elect an *economic representative*, possibly a deputy General Secretary, with responsibility for economics and finance.

Even if such considerations and reflections still seem to be a long way down the road, it will be in the framework of the Convention, due to report in the next year or so, that the underlying institutional and structural foundations for euro area co-ordination and representation have to be laid. Hence the issue is very much a 'live' one.

Conclusions

What this institutional struggle for participation and influence clearly demonstrates is:

- The lack of will on the part of member states to accept that the euro area has become an international player in its own right *replacing national interest with a European common interest.* National vanities still prevail;

- A lack of trust and worries that the delegation of monetary and fiscal decisions to a common representative might lead to national welfare losses;

- The lack of acceptance of the necessity to determine an optimal or, at least feasible, aggregate fiscal and macro-economic stance vis-à-vis the US and Japan.

These problems highlight the fundamental weakness of the European approach. Since Europe did not start out by forging a common consensual Economic and Fiscal Policy model, but rather decided to launch the project of a single currency and monetary integration in the face of different national 'philosophies' of economic policy-making, in the hope that a unionised monetary policy would force macro economic policy convergence upon the participant governments, we are confronted today with all kinds of co-ordination problems. In a sense it is true: the tail is wagging the dog and this implies co-ordination costs.

Therefore, a strong European decision taking authority in finance and economics seems indispensable, as does a genuine European economic advisory capability. However, enough leeway has to be reserved at the level of national economic policy-making to make sure that deals and ideals are in equilibrium. Monetary Union should not, even implicitly, *impose* models of economic governance on EU member states. It is rather on the basis of continuous discourse and exchange, i.e. through a voluntary approach, that we will be able to mould our European economy into a coherent and powerful entity.

References

Alesina A., Blanchard O., Gali J., Giavazzi, F. & Uhlig H. (2001) *Defining a Macroeconomic Framework for the Euro Area: Monitoring the European Central Bank 3,* London: CEPR.

Buti, M. & Sapir, A. eds. (1998) *Economic Policy Making in EMU,* Oxford: Oxford University Press.

Commission (2002) *A Project for Europe,* communication no. 247, 22 May, Brussels: European Commission.

Collignon, S. (2001) 'Economic Policy Coordination in EMU: Institutional and Political Requirements', May 2001, paper presented at the Center for European Studies, Harvard University.

Feldstein, M. (1988) *International Economic Cooperation,* Chigaco: University Press.

Frenkel, J.A. & Rockett, R.E. (1988) 'International Macroeconomic Policy Co-ordination when Policymakers do not Agree on the True Model', in *AER,* vol. 76.

Hagen von, J. & Mundschenk, S. (2001) 'The Functioning of Economic Policy Coordination', mimeograph, Bonn.

Jacquet, P. & Pisani-Ferry, J. (2000) 'La coordination des politiques economiques dans la zone Euro', *Questions européennes,* January, 2001.

Korkman, S. (2002) 'Fiscal Policy Co-ordination in EMU', in Brunila, A., Buti, M. and Franco, D. (eds.) *The Stability and Growth Pact: The Architecture of Fiscal Policy in EMU,* London: Macmillan.

Kotz, H.H. (1996) 'How Trade, Financial and Monetary Integration Interact', University of Toronto, mimeograph.

Moravcsik, A. (1993) 'Preferences and Power in the European Union', *Journal of Common Market Studies,* vol. 31.

Siebert, M. (1997) 'Zu den Voraussetzungen den Europäischen Währungsunion', Kiel, *Discussion Paper 289,* Institut für Weltwirtschaft.

Solbes, P. (2002) *Economic Policy Co-ordination – the Way Forward,* 2 May, mimeograph, Brussels Economic Forum.

The Implications of Structural Economic Change for European Policies

Diane Coyle

Introduction

Every generation feels that it lives in unusually exciting and turbulent times, a natural sense of self-importance which invites the inevitable scepticism about whether the world is fundamentally any different. This dynamic has been clear in the debate about whether there is a 'new economy,' the handy shorthand for underlying change in the structure of the leading economies. A burst of new economy enthusiasm generated by the US economic boom and the dot.com exuberance has given way to doubts about what, if anything, is really 'new.'

It would be a mistake to take this scepticism too far. After all, the cluster of technologies attaining commercial viability between about 1985 and 2015 is extraordinary. It includes not just the high-profile information and communications technologies, but others based on the unprecedented decline in the cost of data-processing: biotechnology, advanced materials, nanotechnology, robotics. They clearly have the potential to accomplish what radical technologies always have, a dramatic qualitative improvement in human well-being. It would be surprising indeed if an annual average growth rate of 56 per cent over 40 years (so far) in computational power turned out to have no significant impact.

Picking through the economic evidence, mostly applying to the United States, does indeed lead to the conclusion that there has been important structural change. To put it as cautiously as possible, there has been a clear structural break in a number of important macroeconomic time series patterns such as the link between unemployment and inflation, or the variability of GDP growth, or the trend rate of total factor productivity growth. These point to underlying microeconomic changes, which are confirmed by a growing body of case study evidence. (Blanchard and Simon 2001, McKinsey 2001)

The aim of this essay is to consider how far Europe has gone down this path and what kinds of policy co-ordination might be necessary at the structural level in future. Supply-side improvements are a vital element in the successful co-ordination of monetary and fiscal policy under the single currency, for without the lubrication of productivity gains it will be more difficult to deliver appropriate interest rate levels and budget deficits. Successive summits, at Cardiff, Lisbon and Barcelona, have emphasised the importance of structural change for the future prosperity of European citizens, but their practical results still lag behind the ambitions set out by political leaders.

There is, as yet, only a little macroeconomic evidence of any similar changes in most European economies. For example, Finland has enjoyed rapid non-inflationary growth, and clearly has attained leadership in some high-tech industries. The UK looks to have achieved a similar improvement to the US in its level of unemployment consistent with stable inflation, but its productivity performance has not improved. However, across the Continent as a whole neither the statistical nor the anecdotal evidence suggests there has been significant structural change. (OECD, 2000)

That the experience should be different in different countries is not really such a puzzle. After all, many countries around the world have not yet managed to adopt very old technologies like electricity. Historical examples show that the diffusion of new technologies always depends on the context: on prevailing economic conditions, on extensive complementary investments including social and institutional changes, and on a favourable regulatory framework. As Nathan Rosenberg and Manuel Trachtenberg put it: 'general purpose technologies induce the widespread and more efficient relocation of economic activity, which in turn fosters long-term growth.' This is a slow and disruptive process which imposes costs on some groups in society.

Thus old technologies can remain profitable for long periods after a replacement innovation occurs; or new technologies can require substantial reorganisation and reskilling before they deliver any efficiencies; or legislation and other government interventions may be needed to encourage widespread adoption (David 1991). Change is all the harder at a time of great uncertainty, when nobody can be sure which technologies will succeed in future, and when the statistics and evidence on important aspects of the 'new' economy are incomplete.

This means there is a very real sense in which the existence of a new economy is self-fulfilling. Only if businesses and individuals believe it will be worth making the additional, disruptive investments (in more education, in business reorganisation), and only if governments believe it worth engaging in the political debate needed to adopt new forms of regulation and social organisation, will the new technologies be able to deliver their full potential. My aim in this essay is to outline what kinds of policy in Europe will be needed to encourage and support the possibility of structural change.

The US example

Although some economists and commentators like to pour scorn on the claims of 'newness' in the American economy, the evidence that something about it is different is now overwhelming. It takes three forms:

- An increase in the trend rate of productivity growth since about 1990, compared with the lacklustre trend growth rate of the 1970s and 80s. The extent of the pick-up is still hotly debated – with disagreement about its aggregate size and its spread outside a few leading sectors of the economy. It will be some years before there are enough data points to resolve the debate. Nevertheless, it is now clear there has been an improvement in the trend.

- An improved macroeconomic performance: more stable growth, thanks to reduced inventory-sales ratios and low inflation; and a fall in the non-accelerating inflation rate of unemployment. Again, the econometric evidence of a structural break is clear (Blanchard and Simon 2001).

- Case studies confirming the existence of substantial productivity gains in industries and businesses which are both heavy users of new technologies and have made significant changes in their business processes (McKinseys 2001). Examples include retailing, logistics, finance, and durable manufacturing. It is the existence of numerous examples that explain why so many Americans were so enthusiastic about the new economy, and remain so despite the recession: it is something millions of them have experienced in their daily life. It has changed what they do and how they do it.

So despite continuing academic controversy, the US has something that can, for the sake of argument, be labelled a new economy. In Europe, on the other hand, it is equally clear that we do not. There are of course success stories, mainly in smaller economies such as Ireland, Finland and Sweden. But, as research at the OECD and elsewhere has documented, few European economies display a productivity pick-up or improved labour market tradeoffs.

There is little argument about the reason, either: the need for further structural reform of the European economies. This has been a policy priority since at least the March 2000 European Council summit in Lisbon, when Europe's leaders set themselves the aim of turning the EU into the world's most competitive, knowledge-based and sustainable economy within a decade. The March 2002 summit in Barcelona reiterated the ambition and agreed a number of further measures such as liberalisation of the energy market for big commercial customers.

The policy agenda confirmed in Barcelona is therefore familiar by now (although many observers were disappointed with the lack of concrete progress at the summit):

- Liberalisation of the nationally-framed markets in energy, air travel, telecommunications and finance.

- Labour market reforms to boost the employment rate, which remains very low in a number of member countries.

- Measures to promote particular high-tech industries such as biotechnology, where the EU has smaller and younger companies than the US and lags well behind in measures of innovation like numbers of international patents filed.

Biotechnology is a good example of what's at stake for the EU. It is the world's biggest market, and will account for half of a global market for biotech products likely to be worth some 200bn euro by 2010; but Europe could end up depending on imports from the US unless a native industry can be grown, in the face of a vocal opposition campaign, from clusters of activity in Germany, the UK, France, Denmark, Sweden, Belgium and the Netherlands. The United States is dominant in terms of leading biotech companies; but, unlike other new technologies, in biotechnology and genomics Europe has a science base that can rival the American universities. There is real hope of getting to the technological frontier in this area, in contrast to computer science, say.

The Commission is proposing spending 2.15bn euro on research in the next genomics research programme running from January 2003. It will present a regular Life Sciences and Biotechnology Report, and draw up a rolling work programme for related legislation. The Commission will then review the consistency of EU policies and legislation affecting life sciences and biotechnology. However, the industry exemplifies very clearly some of the characteristics of the new technology-based economy that pose particular policy challenges. The EU will need policies that are correct as well as consistent.

The key structural policy issues

I want to focus on aspects of policy that relate specifically to new economy questions. This ignores other important aspects of structural reform in Europe such as continuing labour market rigidities in some member economies, pension reform and completion of the single market in a number of areas. However, these issues are well understood and have been thoroughly discussed elsewhere. Instead, here I sketch the big issues arising from the need to create an economic structure that will support the adoption and diffusion of promising new technologies, and compare the American and European policy positions. They are: the efficient scale of activity; competition; intellectual property; the science base; immigration; finance and regulation. Some of these have received attention from policy makers already, but not necessarily in this context, while others have been peripheral to the core economic policy debate. An appreciation of the linkages between the different aspects of policy affecting future productivity growth would both help specific policies evolve in the most fruitful direction and also help inspire the nitty-gritty of debate about rather technical areas with a vision of what prize the process as a whole could deliver.

Increasing returns to scale

Scale has long been a source of competitive advantage to American industries, ranging from steel and aerospace all the way to finance and movies. Comparative studies such as those carried out over many years by the National Institute of Economic and Social Research suggest increasing returns to scale play an important part in explaining the past US productivity lead over the EU. In new economy industries, increasing returns to scale due to high start-up and fixed costs and close-to-zero marginal costs will be more than ever the canonical industrial structure. One reason is that many new economy industries display network effects, whereby the product or service is more valuable to its consumers the more consumers there are, like mobile telephones or a particular software standard. Another is that the initial research and development costs in many modern industries are so significant, and the returns to being first in the market and achieving a technological 'lock-in' are so great (Arthur, 1989). John Sutton (2000) has described the strategic game between firms in cutting-edge industries as an 'arms race,' in which each needs to spend a growing amount on R&D to survive. This implies *increasing* returns to scale.

With industrial structure more and more like pharmaceuticals or software, less and less like textiles or food processing, business profitability will depend on access to as large a market as possible. Past estimates of the benefits of the creation of a single market are probably understated. What's more, it is not only a genuine European market that matters, but also access to the global market. The benefits of openness and trade will be greater than ever. Anything EU governments can do to extend the size of markets by reducing barriers and frictions will be crucial. Apart from anything else, this consideration puts enlargement in a fresh perspective, as a natural extension to the domestic market.

Competition

Network industries and increasing returns to scale raise questions for competition policy. Again, in a simple comparison with the US the EU does not come off too well. In both economies the attitude of the authorities has ebbed and flowed over time but US anti-monopoly legislation and practice has been consistently tougher as far as the domestic behaviour of American companies is concerned. The pay-off in terms of lower prices to consumers and higher productivity and more profitable firms is clear.

To take a recent example, retailing is one of the US industries demonstrating the biggest productivity gains during the 1990s. The reason appears to be that the industry leader, WalMart, set the pace in terms of technology adoption, business re-engineering and price-cutting, while the high degree of competition in the sector spread the same changes rapidly to other companies.

However, competition policy is likely to become increasingly challenging. In an industry with high fixed costs and low marginal costs there will be a strong tendency towards monopoly. In high-tech businesses it is the 'winner-takes-all' phenomenon best illustrated by Microsoft. The public policy problem involves trading off an adequate reward for innovation by permitting a temporary monopoly, against preventing abuse of a dominant market position to keep out present and future competition. Effective competition is likely to take the form of technical innovation, with successive generations of products replacing each other, as it is very hard to sustain static competition in an industry with very high increasing returns to scale. The definitions of the scope of the market or the transition from one generation of product to another are highly technical and contentious, as the Microsoft case so well demonstrates.

Intellectual property

This leads on to questions about the appropriate framework for protecting intellectual property. Property rights are the DNA of successful capitalist economies, but it is unlikely that the legal framework for their protection dating from the 19th century will be appropriate for the protection of intellectual property, increasingly important as a source of value.

Many technology experts believe the US government has gone too far, with the Digital Millennium Copyright Act, in treating 'knowledge' as just like any other property, and they fear over-strong protection of intellectual copyright is inhibiting the sharing of knowledge and future innovation (Lessig 2001). For one thing, the marginal cost of distributing knowledge is close to zero. For another, intellectual property, unlike physical property, is non-excludable in consumption, a characteristic it shares with many public goods such as clean air. The externality implies there will tend to be a sub-optimal level of private investment in 'knowledge' (understood as intellectual property in any form). Government actions should be aimed at encouraging, rather than inhibiting, the transmission of knowledge from one person to another.

While we know that competition in a reasonably free market is the best way to stimulate applied innovation, it is not clear how to make this work in the case of information goods. In fact, there is a strong case for arguing that some forms of intellectual property are in fact outright public goods, in cases where they act as de facto standards. Computer operating systems might be one example. Our understanding of the appropriate regulation and legal framework is in its infancy.

At the same time, the intellectual property framework clearly needs to provide an adequate reward to knowledge-creation over time. This is the patents problem, where a deliberate restriction on the free flow of knowledge is designed to allow an innovator to reap those rewards. But even though this trade-off appears straightforward it is not always well-understood.

Take the example of the pricing of anti-Aids drugs in developing countries. Pharmaceuticals companies argued that their patents allowed them to charge a high price in all their markets, and justified this by their need to continue innovating. But there is no reason why the companies should appropriate all the gains from the opening of new markets to their products, rather than share the gains with new consumers in the form of much lower prices. The only requirement to preserve their incentives to innovate is that the drugs are not shipped back from developing countries to undercut prices in their initial developed country markets. However, the appropriate policy will vary depending on the product and the links between the markets in which it is sold (CEPR, 2002).

In this area there is a great opportunity for the EU, whose governments and people anyway have a much stronger sense of the value of public goods, to improve on the American model in designing property rights appropriate for the new economy. The example of the Human Genome Project, a public effort in Europe and a private effort in the United States, is a good symbol of the difference in approach. Governments may need to vastly increase the extent of their support for basic science anyway. They may need to consider purchasing patents for the benefit of the public, especially in the case of medical innovations. In short, the European model could well prove a more efficient solution to the problems of intellectual property given the prevalence of externalities in knowledge.

The science base

In many areas of knowledge, especially in the sciences, the United States has a substantial lead in research excellence. The reason this could matter for the European economy is that clusters of high-technology industry tend to form around universities. The exchange and testing of the complicated and subtle ideas on which business development in these industries depends so heavily is very much a matter of face-to-face contact and personal networks. This is why geographical clustering seems even more pronounced in the new economy than the old.

Again, this argument calls for European governments to redouble their efforts to encourage academic excellence. Generous funding for basic research programmes at specialist centres is one option. There are more indirect routes, too, such as considering tax incentives for private and charitable donations to universities. American institutions have a tremendous financial advantage in the form of the strong culture of alumni and charitable donations to universities.

Scientific excellence rests on cultural foundations too. Having centres of excellence implies an elitism which sits uncomfortably with the stronger European egalitarianism of outcomes. Straightforward anti-scientific sentiments also have a stronger policy impact in Europe – although the trends in the US may be heading in the same direction with the spread of creationism and the recent block on developing new lines of stem cells for research.

Immigration

Openness is crucial to new economy success in several ways, including access to bigger markets. It also matters in the subtler way of openness to new ideas and ways of thinking. Diversity of the workforce is a tremendous advantage in innovation and problem solving (Weitzmann, 1998).

Europe has been slow in recognising that immigration can be anything other than an economic and social burden. Yet the OECD's research on cross-country differences in productivity performance suggest that the high rate of immigration into the US has been an important source of competitive advantage in recent years. This is clear in the case of Taiwanese and Indian computer experts moving to Silicon Valley or Route 128, but it is a broader advantage (Saxenian, 2002). The increased labour supply all along the range of skills has contributed to the extremely good macroeconomic performance in the US throughout the 1990s.

Nor is there much evidence that immigration has undermined real wages for the unskilled, as immigrants tend to move to very tight labour markets. The groups in the US that have experienced real wage declines have been those in areas of technological redundancy, like the old steel belt, or those with the multiple and self-reinforcing economic and social disadvantages of living in inner city ghettos.

Regulation

Part of the recipe for America's relative new economy success is its flexibility and the light regulatory touch of government. Rigid control, hierarchy, planning and centralisation have been profoundly undermined by the new technological paradigm – most spectacularly in the extreme case of the former planned economies, but the point goes much wider.

It is clear that the desirable government policies to underpin economic success have changed. There is no such thing as a market in the abstract. All markets are shaped by regulation and legislation as well as culture and history, and work well or badly according to their underlying structure. Brad DeLong and Lawrence Summers (2001) highlight a number of policies as being crucial to the success of the original industrial revolution, such as the enclosure legislation in Britain, limited liability, US anti-trust policy and the abolition of barriers to trade between states. The question is what sort of institutional and legal framework European governments should be working towards in order to create the right conditions and incentives for growth. It will be very different from the US framework, but there will nevertheless be useful lessons in areas such as competition in network industries or the development of venture capital.

Indeed, the role of government is likely to be more important than ever in the new economy. This is because of its pervasive economies of scale and externalities, because of the need for new infrastructure, for a different form of education for the workforce and because of the importance of openness which will depend heavily on intra-governmental agreements to work properly. At the same time, many European governments need to unwind their traditional intervention in business to ensure they are not standing in the way of enterprise and innovation.

Conclusions

This is not the role we have grown used to, though. European governments – at all levels – need to get beyond opposition to change because it is too 'Anglo-Saxon' or because deregulation has to involve the sacrifice of other ideals of cohesion. And the challenge is not just one of designing the right policies in a technical sense but also in bringing to voters an ideal of dynamism and prosperity. It is a question of confidence.

There is absolutely no inevitability about the new economy, which will turn out however we collectively act to shape it. It might not happen at all, in Europe or elsewhere. It will almost certainly take a different shape in the EU than the US, given our different history and political preferences.

There is nevertheless tremendous potential for Europe to grasp the opportunity to shape a better future for all its citizens, however. The euro and enlargement offer scope for rapid growth by extending the size of the single market and increasing the scope for capturing economies of scale.

European preferences for stronger government and high-quality public sector activities might well turn out to be advantages, at least in those new economy industries where there are significant knowledge spillovers and externalities.

Structural change is always highly disruptive, and many of the policy issues are intrinsically difficult because they are so politically sensitive. It is also in the nature of most microeconomic policies that they involve detailed and technical debates. In many areas achieving agreement between member countries over the appropriate policies will be difficult. Reform is bound to be piecemeal and incremental.

Nevertheless it is important for the politicians to keep up the momentum in the structural reform process, despite the slow progress so far. A stronger European economy would be very much in the interests of the rest of the world, for the sake of economic balance and as a counterweight to American political influence, as well as in the interests of all Europeans. Failure to take advantage of the opportunity for faster productivity growth offered by new technologies will also make the co-ordination of macroeconomic policy within monetary union harder, by exacerbating the possible tensions between monetary and fiscal policy whenever the Euro area economy slows.

References

Arthur, B. (1989) 'Competing technologies, increasing returns and lock-in by historical events', *Economic Journal*, pp. 116-131.

Blanchard, O. & Simon, J. (2001) *The Long and Large Decline in US Output Volatility*, Brookings Papers on Economic Activity.

CEPR (2001) 'Report on globalisation prepared for European Commission', May, London: CEPR.

Coyle, D. (1997) *The Weightless World*, Capstone.

Coyle, D. (2001) *Paradoxes of Prosperity*, Texere.

David, P. (1991) *Computer and Dynamo: The Modern Productivity Paradox in a Not-too-distant Mirror*, in Technology and productivity, OECD.

DeLong, B. & Summers, L. (2001) *The New Economy: Background, Questions, Speculations*, August, Harvard University working paper, available at http://www.j-bradford-delong.net http://www.j-bradforddelong.net

Lessig, L. (2001) *The Future of Ideas*, Random House.

McKinsey Global Institute (2001) *US Productivity growth 1995-2000*, October, http://www.mkinsey.com/knowledge/mgi

OECD (2000) *Differences in Economic Growth Across the OECD in the 1990s: The Role of Innovation and Information Technologies*, February.

OECD (2000) *Structural Factors Driving Industrial Growth*, April.

Rosenberg, N. & Trachtenberg, M. (2001) 'A General Purpose technology at Work: The Corliss Steam Engine in the late 19th Century US', *NBER Working Paper*, no. 8485, September.

Saxenian, A. L. (2002) 'Brain Circulation: How High-Skill Immigration makes Everyone Better Off', *Brookings Review*, vol. 20, no. 1, pp. 28-31, Winter.

Sutton, L. (2000) *Rich Trades, Scarce Capabilities: Industrial Development revisited*, Keynes Lecture, http://www.res.org.uk.

Weitzmann, M. (1998) 'Recombinant Growth', *Quarterly Journal of Economics*, CXIII, no. 2, pp. 331-360, May.

Ageing and public pension reforms in the European Union: Common patterns, common concern?

Jacques Le Cacheux[*]

Introduction

The final communiqué of the March 2002 Barcelona European Summit mentions the common goal of postponing the average effective retirement age in the EU member states. This decision follows a series of moves, starting with the Luxembourg, Cardiff and Lisbon Summits, to launch a common employment strategy, with the objective of raising national employment rates, and the inclusion in the Broad Economic Policy Guidelines (BEPG) of a general statement in favour of pension reform. These developments may seem to be at odds with the subsidiarity principle, inasmuch as employment and social policies had, till then, been considered to be the exclusive realm of national governments. The increasing encroachments of EU-level decision-making in such fields, when they are deemed to be of common concern, are the major examples of a new EU approach to policy co-ordination in areas that are adjudged to be of common concern, but are not explicitly covered in the Treaties, giving rise to the so-called 'open method of co-ordination'.

This chapter deals with the macroeconomics of pension reform in the European Union and tries to address the issues of overall consequences of

* This paper draws on work carried out in the INGENUE project, as well as work of various researchers at OFCE, in particular for the *Rapport sur l'état de l'Union européenne 2002*. Special thanks to the INGENUE Team.

major options, as well as the rationale for bringing national pension reforms into a common, European framework, and for co-ordinating or even harmonising pension schemes. The first two sections of the chapter present a summary assessment of the demographic situation and prospects, and of the labour market developments that bear on the financial position of pay-as-you-go, public pension schemes in Europe. The third section briefly reviews the major reform plans that have been undertaken or contemplated in European countries. Section 4 summarises the conclusions of a number of recent studies on the macroeconomic consequences of pension reforms, first in the closed-economy, then in the open-economy and world analytical framework, emphasising the global dimension of population ageing and pension reform. A concluding section discusses possible risks from the combination of market integration, competition and widely divergent national pension schemes, and the rationale for co-ordinating pension reforms in the EU.

Common trends and differences in population ageing

As is well known, population ageing is, to a very large extent, a trend common to all EU members. It results from the combination of two demographic factors: the sharp fall in fertility that affected all European countries after 1975, but with marked differences across countries; and the progressive lengthening of life expectancy, a phenomenon observed in most developed countries, though with some variations too. The current European ageing process is itself the outcome of two distinct components: the above-mentioned, persistent trend towards longer life expectancy, and a transitory component, resulting from the baby-boom-baby-bust profile of fertility rates in the decades following World-War-II, a succession that also shows a fair amount of variation across countries.

In the EU as a whole, the old-age dependency ratio – i.e. the ratio of the population over 60 to the 20-60, working-age population – will roughly double between 2000 and 2050, according to UN demographic projections: from 39.5 per cent to 79.5 per cent (Table 1). Due to the baby-boom-baby-bust effect, much of this surge will happen between 2000 and 2030 or 2040, depending on each country's specific circumstances.

Though a common fate of all European countries – and, indeed of, developed countries in general, especially Japan where it is even more pronounced, population ageing will occur at different dates, and to different degrees in the various countries of the EU. Some, like Italy and Sweden, already have fairly high old-age dependency ratios and will reach 50 per cent or more before 2010; in others, such as Germany and Greece, current ratios are high, but the 50 per cent threshold will be passed between 2010 and 2020, as it will in a majority of EU countries. The exceptions are Austria and Portugal where this happens later, and Ireland where the big increases only happen after 2030. The other major difference in ageing profiles is the level reached by old-age dependency ratios by the year 2050: it will still be moderate – below 80 per cent, the EU average – in a majority of countries, but is likely to be around 100 per cent in Southern European countries: Greece, Italy and Spain.

Table 1. Old-age dependency ratios

	1995	2000	2005	2010	2020	2030	2040	2050
Austria	34.1	35.7	36.7	39.6	47.9	64.8	77.3	83.0
Belgium	39.0	39.3	39.9	43.8	54.7	71.2	73.4	74.9
Denmark	35.6	35.9	39.5	45.2	52.7	63.0	66.5	61.7
Finland	34.1	35.7	38.3	46.5	59.3	68.0	67.2	67.7
France	37.4	37.8	38.2	42.8	52.7	61.1	66.6	68.0
Germany	36.5	41.7	44.4	45.2	54.1	72.6	73.9	75.9
Greece	40.8	44.0	44.7	47.8	55.8	69.5	88.2	97.3
Ireland	29.0	28.1	28.7	31.4	39.2	45.4	55.1	61.8
Italy	40.2	43.3	45.7	50.0	59.8	80.9	98.1	97.2
Luxembourg	33.7	34.6	35.9	38.9	48.7	60.6	67.4	69.3
Netherlands	30.9	31.9	34.6	40.5	52.9	71.3	77.6	76.0
Portugal	37.1	37.6	38.5	41.3	47.4	58.9	79.0	84.1
Spain	38.4	38.5	39.5	42.1	51.4	70.4	97.9	106.0
Sweden	41.9	42.0	45.7	51.3	58.6	68.9	71.7	73.8
UK	38.6	38.9	40.3	44.1	51.1	62.7	64.6	66.7
EU15	**37.6**	**39.5**	**41.4**	**44.6**	**53.6**	**68.6**	**77.2**	**79.5**
Japan	36.5	41.4	47.7	57.5	65.6	72.4	85.3	86.2
USA	30.0	29.8	30.8	33.9	45.0	53.0	53.9	56.4

*60 and over/20-60
(*Source:* UN, 1999).

Current situation and prospects for pay-as-you-go public pension systems

Population ageing is, of course, a major challenge for welfare systems, and especially for retirement pension schemes.[1] But the difficulty is much lesser in a funded system with defined contributions, be it public or private. However, insofar as European countries all have public retirement pension systems that are based, at least to some extent, on pay-as-you-go principles, the strain on pension systems is likely to be considerable, which explains the insistence of the European Commission and Council on the necessity and urgency of reforming public pension schemes.

In pay-as-you-go pension systems with defined benefits, the burden of contribution falls entirely on the currently employed population, the more so, for a given level of the replacement rate, the higher the number of beneficiaries of the system. The relevant measure of this financial burden is therefore not so much the age-dependency ratios themselves (Table 1), but these ratios corrected for employment rates (Table 2). Taking this indicator of the labour market situation of the various European countries makes the current financing prospects of the pension systems look even worse and, to some extent widens the differences amongst countries. In particular, it widens the gap between, especially, the Nordic countries, but also, to some extent, Portugal, UK and the Netherlands, that have relatively mild ageing profiles in the coming decades and enjoy above-average overall employment rates, and Southern EU members – Italy and Spain – where the labour market situation aggravates already bleak demographic prospects. Looking just at employment rates, Belgium, Greece, France and Germany are in an intermediate position.

An additional factor is relatively low labour market participation rates for people over 55, a fairly common feature that has long been encouraged by governments trying to fight unemployment by reducing the labour supply, especially through early retirement schemes and financial incentives to withdraw from the labour market. Indeed, in most European countries, activity rates are very low at ages 55-65, making the average effective retirement age significantly lower than the legal retirement age. Here again though, there are presently significant cross-country differences, with the UK and Scandinavian countries standing out in the upper range and Belgium at the bottom.

The outcome of this combination of (on average) fairly generous pay-as-you-go public pension schemes, low employment rates, and high and rising age-dependency ratios is an overall high share of pensions – especially pay-as-you-go, public pension schemes – in GDP in all EU countries, though again with marked differences.

Table 2. *Employment and activity rates*

	Overall employment rates (1998)	Activity rates (1999)	
		55-60	60-65
Austria	75.1	44.0	10.8
Belgium	63.1	39.8	13.3
Denmark	83.5	74.6	35.3
Finland	71.5	62.5	23.2
France	65.8	59.3	15.6
Germany	71.7	65.1	20,9
Greece	64.1	49.9	33.3
Ireland*	70.4	45.6	
Italy	57.9	50.2	19.6
Luxembourg	66.3	NA	NA
Netherlands	77.2	49.7	15.9
Portugal	79.4	56.4	45.1
Spain	57.9	51.2	27.6
Sweden*	80.3	68.6	
UK	79.6	65.5	37.6
EU15	**69.1**		
Japan		76.7	56.9
USA		70.1	46.8

* For Ireland and Sweden, the activity rate shown is for age cohort 55-65.
Sources: Eurostat and OECD.

Reform options

Given these labour market realities and demographic trends, the EU countries all face serious financing problems for their welfare states in general and for pay-as-you-go public retirement schemes in particular, albeit with varying degrees of urgency and seriousness depending on the specifics of the ageing process and of the rules governing the public pension system in each country. To elucidate what is at stake and to put the various reform options facing EU governments in context, it is useful to look at three policy parameters: the duration of contributions needed to obtain a full-rate pension – which affects the age of retirement – the contribution rate (as a percentage of the earnings of the currently working population), and the replacement rate (the pension as a percentage of earnings, which may be expressed as a ratio of last earnings, or of the earnings of currently working population, or another reference-point. In combination, these three parameters determine the generosity of the pay-as-you-go pension scheme; their interaction with demographic and labour-market changes determines the average internal rate of return of the pension scheme for individuals, as well as the overall financial burden of the scheme, assuming its budget balances on a yearly basis.[2]

The are essentially three reform options:

- The first is the status-quo for retirees, in relative, standard-of-living terms – namely leaving the length of the contribution period and the replacement rate unchanged – which implies that the contribution rate will, in future, have to be increased in line with the rise in the age-dependency ratio (number of retirees as a percentage of working population) in order to balance the budget of the public pension fund;

- The second is a reduction in the generosity of the system for retirees – i.e. cutting the replacement rate, either by a pre-determined amount or by blocking the contribution rate and letting the replacement rate adjust endogenously;

- The third is to lengthen the contribution period, which effectively means keeping the ratio of retirement time over working time approximately constant as life expectancy increases.

In recent years, many European countries have based pension reforms on one of these three options or a mix of all three. Most prominently, Germany in 2001 announced and launched a sweeping reform that will cap the contribution rate at a level slightly above the present one while letting future pensions adjust downwards as the age-dependency ratio increases. Workers will also be offered incentives to raise their retirement incomes by accumulating savings in financial institutions that will be specially authorised by the federal government, enabling them to benefit from associated tax and other privileges.

Italy and Sweden have chosen to reform the public pension system principally by establishing a close link between individual contributions and the amount of the pension entitlement. These mechanisms in effect guarantee a rate of return for individuals within the public pension fund, thus doing away with the redistribution that had been an explicit feature of the former system.

France, which is often portrayed as the only country in Europe that has not reformed its social security system, has so far relied on progressively reducing the replacement rate and lengthening the contribution period, but only for private sector workers: the 1993 reform, enacted under the Balladur government, has enshrined the unofficial practice of indexing pensions to prices (rather than wages) into the law, with the consequence that pension replacement rates in the private sector are being progressively eroded as yearly price increases are slightly below wage rises.[3] In addition, the reference period for calculating the pension has been extended from the ten years with the highest wage income to the twenty-five years with the highest wage income, the intention being again to automatically reduce the replacement rate.

Macroeconomic consequences of pension reforms

Reforming pensions effectively means changing the outlook for income and consumption of those currently of working age as well as future generations. According to the life-cycle hypothesis, it therefore alters the consumption-saving decisions of all those affected by the new regime, as soon as the reform plan is announced. These changes in turn will have macroeconomic consequences on growth, incomes, employment, etc., that have been analysed in many recent studies in the various countries. The conclusions vary considerably according to the analytical framework being used.

Reasoning in autarky

Most existing attempts at quantifying the macroeconomic consequences of population ageing and possible reforms of public retirement schemes have been carried out within the analytical framework of the closed economy. Some, admittedly crude, assessments simply extrapolate current macroeconomic trends on a national basis, and take ageing into account simply by changing the assumed profile of population cohorts – mostly dependency ratios and activity rates – in the future. Though they have been extensively relied upon in national policy debates on public retirement pension schemes, such studies, based on exogenous growth and households' behaviour, may at best provide a rough idea of the order of the magnitude of required increases in contribution rates compared with a counterfactual of unchanged pension schemes. This is highly unlikely: indeed the combination of population ageing with existing retirement arrangements would, in many countries, induce a considerable and long-lasting rise in contribution rates that most analysts would deem unacceptably high. In those countries that have already enacted reforms of their public pension systems, the new rules are often found to be imperfect in many ways, and in particular, to result in increased inequalities amongst pensioners, and sometimes in a very marked decline in average replacement rates that cannot possibly be sustained for very long. But apart from showing the unsustainable character of current practices, such mechanical evaluations are not of much interest.

Recent, more sophisticated research has taken account of the induced effects of pension prospects and reforms on individual decisions to work, consume and save from a life-cycle perspective. These analyses, in the spirit of Feldstein's (1974) pioneering work, are usually conducted in the framework of a closed-economy, overlapping-generations, general equilibrium model. They show that the status-quo scenario, in which replacement rates are assumed unchanged and contribution rates are allowed to rise to balance the accounts of the pay-as-you-go public pension scheme, is even worse than depicted in the simple macroeconomic projections. Indeed, the increasing contribution rates, with constant replacement rates, imply a fall in labour supply (in those models where it is endogenous and responsive to net wages or net take-home pay) and, above all, a fall in individual saving that, in the aggregate, reduces capital accumulation and growth.[4] In such models, switching to individual capitalisation, by curtailing the public, pay-as-you-go pension schemes, is always beneficial in aggregate, because per-capita output is a decreasing function of the capital intensity of production which is, itself, a simple, increasing function of the real rate of return on productive capital, i.e. the real interest rate. Moving from an unfunded pension system to a funded one will therefore generally induce some redistribution amongst cohorts, because some will have to pay twice. But the overall effect on consumption is beneficial, as per-capita output is higher, so that winners can, in principle, compensate the losing generations for the fall in consumption the latter have to bear.

Perhaps surprisingly, postponing the legal retirement age may not have unambiguously positive aggregate effects in closed-economy models. Indeed, one obvious consequence of this reform is to increase the total working time of individuals over their life cycle, which entails higher lifetime incomes, and hence higher lifetime consumption; but it also cuts into – admittedly forced – leisure, which will have a cost in terms of individual welfare. In addition, whereas the resulting increase in labour supply will, in equilibrium, generate more aggregate output in the economy, it will also require more capital. This higher demand for capital may or may not be matched by a higher supply, i.e. more aggregate saving: the income effect is positive, but there also is a negative effect on individual saving, namely the shortening of the retirement period, which ought to reduce accumulation for the purpose of financing retirement consumption. If the latter effect dominates, the interest rate will be higher and hence the capital intensity of the economy will decrease, meaning that average labour productivity will be lower as well.

European pension reforms in a global context

However, analysing these pension reforms as if Europe were a closed economy is misleading. Indeed, financial globalisation is precisely about widening the range of possible intertemporal exchanges amongst individuals by opening up new investment opportunities abroad. Since changes in aggregate saving and/ or aggregate investment in one region of the world are no longer bottled up in that same region, the induced consequences on equilibrium interest rates will be different, hence also the feedback effects on individual incomes and on saving incentives. When European pension reforms are inscribed into the global picture of world economic and financial equilibrium, their induced effects on interest rates will be smaller than in the closed-economy context, as part of it will dissipate in a much larger world capital market, even if Europe is not exactly a 'small open economy', hence changes in European aggregate saving and investment have consequences for the world capital market equilibrium. In particular, financial openness means that European domestic saving and investment do not have to balance.[5] It becomes possible for the various regions of the world to run current account surpluses or deficits to smooth fluctuations over time, very much in the same way as individuals may smooth their consumption profile over the life cycle if they are able to accumulate and borrow.

Considered in this broader context, the pension problem of Europe appears in a different light.[6] First, population ageing is a world phenomenon, but with significant regional differences: Japan and Western Europe may be broadly characterised by the combination of advanced, secular lengthening of life expectancy and a significant transitory component corresponding to the baby-boom/baby-bust scenario of the second half of the 20th century; North America appears to have a relatively larger young population and a much less sharp baby-boom/baby-bust profile; and all other regions of the world seem to have embarked much later on their demographic transition, with China being the most advanced, followed by India, Brazil, etc., and with sub-Saharan Africa lagging far behind.[7] That countries are facing different ageing patterns is a source of opportunities for mutually beneficial intertemporal exchanges: regions with high saving rates and relatively low investment needs can run current account surpluses, hence exporting capital to regions with comparatively low saving rates and high investment demand. It may even be argued that this is what financial globalisation is all about.

In addition to demographics, two other major differences amongst regions of the world bear on the macroeconomics of population ageing and pension reforms: inequalities in economic development, as captured, for instance, by total factor productivity, itself a function of several variables including capital intensity of production; and discrepancies in national social security systems. Indeed, due to the former, and notwithstanding other differences and impediments, international capital will flow from countries with relatively higher capital intensity to less developed regions, characterised by both lower capital intensity – hence higher marginal return on productive investment – and larger working-age populations. The generosity and coverage of the social security system will influence private saving and accumulation.

In such an analytical framework, Europe appears to be distinctive on more than one account:

• It is one of the most developed regions of the world, meaning that its capital intensity ratio is high, and the marginal productivity of investment relatively low;

• Its demographic structure is characterised by the double ageing phenomena, described above; and

• It clearly has the most generous public pension schemes, both with relatively short working lives and long retirement periods, and with high replacement rates in most European countries.

Leaving the institutional arrangements unchanged from what they were at the end of the past century would, given the ageing prospects, have entailed a marked increase in the financial burden of social security – and indeed other services provided by the European welfare states – on the employed population, probably leading, in time, to lower aggregate saving rates. In this scenario, Europe would have been a major capital exporter in the first decades of the present century; but it would, after the exhaustion of the baby-boom/baby-bust wave, have turned into a capital importer, due to low saving rates in the second half of the century (INGENUE, 2001).

Even more interesting for our purpose, though, is the finding that financial globalisation somewhat alters the macroeconomic and (intergenerational) distributional consequences of the various pension reform scenarios in Europe. Indeed, in the reform scenarios which entail a less generous pension scheme in the future – through lower replacement rates -, the aggregate saving rate in Europe will be higher. In this case, part of the additional capital accumulation will be exported, so that the rate of return on capital, and hence the real interest rate, will not have to diminish as much as if the European economy were closed: part of the adjustment resulting from pension reform is thus borne by the rest of the world, in a mutually advantageous transaction. Similarly, and even more so, it may be shown (INGENUE, 2001) that postponing the retirement age in Europe has more beneficial aggregate effects for Europe in the global context than in the closed-economy case.

Concluding remarks: globalisation, competition and threats to European welfare states

Although population ageing is common to all European countries, and indeed all regions of the world, arguably as a (happy) consequence of rising standards of living, the timing and precise profile of this process differs markedly from country to country within Europe and between the latter and other regions of the world. Because of existing large and, on average, fairly generous, national public pension systems with, in most European countries, a predominant share of pay-as-you-go, unfunded schemes, population ageing poses a serious challenge in EU countries and several reforms have already been enacted in most member countries. The choice of the reform should be viewed as being essentially a political issue, to be decided within the national policy context. But this chapter has argued that taking explicit account of the openness of the European economies is important to assess the macroeconomic consequences of pensions reform.

For Europe as a whole, the effect of openness arises mostly through the scope for exchange of capital, thus allowing for a disconnection between domestic saving and domestic investment. This opens up opportunities for mutually advantageous intertemporal exchanges with the rest of the world that make consumption smoothing possible at the global level.

Within the EU, however, there are significant differences both in demographics and in retirement schemes, as well as in the way they are financed. Taken together, because pay-as-you-go systems are characterised by a long delay between individual contributions and individual pension benefits, and, in many countries, by some degree of redistribution within generations, there is a danger of tax and social competition amongst member states, as the most mobile fraction of the working age population is composed of precisely those individuals who tend to contribute more than they receive from public pension systems. The modes of financing are also different, with some countries relying mostly on contributions, while others finance public pensions from general taxation. These differences may induce tax-avoidance strategies by the more mobile fraction of the population, thus endangering the most redistributive national systems and forcing all reforms to move in the direction of contributory schemes, actuarially fair and therefore not different from the private, insurance-type pension funds. The desire to prevent such excessive social competition may explain why pension reform has increasingly been recognised as a matter of common concern. Although there is no provision in the treaties for co-ordination in this area, it may be seen as a complement to the more general move to co-ordinate macroeconomic and employment policies.

In any case, because the free movement of persons and workers is a central objective of the treaties and because competition policy is in the hands of the Commission and the European court of justice, the latter is actually building a European jurisprudence on pensions that, if left unattended, will force national governments to clarify the rules governing their systems. It will, thus produce a high degree of harmonisation and hence restrict national policy choices much more effectively than explicit co-ordination.

Finally, a major reason why the theme of pension reforms has featured prominently in the Broad Economic Policy Guidelines from the beginning of EMU, and has recently been included in the field of common interest covered by the open methods of co-ordination, is the fear that failure to reform national pension schemes may lead to macroeconomic, and especially fiscal imbalances that would threaten the objectives of the Stability and Growth Pact, and conceivably the ultimate goal of price stability. But this is, of course, true of almost any national policy; and the heterogeneity of public pension schemes and rules governing the private pensions in EU member States is such that co-ordination is still quite a long way from harmonisation.

Notes

[1] For completeness, it should be added that ageing also has implications for other welfare-related services. In particular, public health services and/or insurance schemes also tend to become more costly as average age increases. This is only partially compensated for by opposite trends in other public and social expenditures, such as family benefits and, though much less apparent, education.

[2] The fear that ageing may, in some countries, lead some governments to run deficits in their pay-as-you-go systems partly explains the involvement of the EU authorities – Commission and Council – in the debate about reforming national pension schemes. A number of countries, including the US and France, have chosen to accumulate financial reserves in a public fund in order to face the bulge in pension spending that will happen with the retirement of baby-boomers. We leave this option aside here and concentrate on 'pure' pay-as-you-go systems, in which the budget of the pension fund is balanced on a yearly basis.

[3] The difference between wage and price yearly increases is the average labour productivity growth rate. Because the latter has been relatively slow over recent years, the yearly reduction in relative purchasing power of pensions has scarcely been noticed. If productivity growth were, for some reason, to accelerate, the gap would widen: hence, paradoxically, the indexing rule means that the more real growth there is in the economy, and the more generous wage increases, the more pensions would lag behind.

[4] For illustrations of such closed economy, overlapping-generations, general-equilibrium models applied to pensions, see, for example: Cazes, Chauveau, Le Cacheux and Loufir, 1992 and 1994.

[5] This is, of course, the intuition behind the celebrated Feldstein and Horioka (1980) analysis of the degree of financial openness.

[6] Some recent analyses of the macroeconomics of pension reforms, such as Turner et al (1998), Reisen (2000) or, more recently, McMorrow and Roeger (2002), have taken the open-economy dimension into account. But they usually only deal with Europe as an open economy and do not explicitly rely on the life-cycle hypothesis. In the INGENUE world model (INGENUE, 2001 and 2002), each region of the world is modeled as an overlapping-generations economy and the demographic assumptions used are the UN projections. All regions are allowed to exchange goods and capital, whereas labour is assumed not to migrate internationally. Thus, there effectively is a world capital market and a single world interest rate at which individual countries will want to lend or borrow according to their saving-investment balance, which is in turn influenced by demographic developments, growth prospects and institutional arrangements for pensions.

[7] The demographic prospects in Africa are not clear, as the uncertainty about demographic transition combines with the deadly consequences of massive epidemics, in particular AIDS.

References

Barr, N. (2000) 'Reforming Pensions: Myths, Truths and Policy Choice', *IMF Working Paper*, August.

Boldrin, M., Dolado, J. J., Jimeno, J. F. & Peracchi, F. (1999) 'The Future of Pensions in Europe', *Economic Policy*, no. 29, October.

Cazes, S., Chauveau, T., Le Cacheux, J. & Loufir, R. (1992) 'An OG Model of the French Economy: Application to the Long-Run Prospects of the Public Pension Scheme', *OFCE Working Papers*, no. 92-5.

Cazes, S., Chauveau, T., Le Cacheux, J. & Loufir, R. (1994) 'Public Pensions in an Overlapping-Generations Model of the French Economy', *Keio Economic Studies*, vol. 31, no. 1.

Chagny, O., Dupont, G., Sterdyniak, H. & Veroni, P. (2001) 'Les réformes des systèmes de retraite en Europe', *Revue de l'OFCE*, no. 78, July.

Esping-Andersen, G., (1996) 'After the Golden Age? Welfare State Dilemmas in a Global Economy', in Esping-Andersen, G. (ed.) *Welfare State in Transition: National Adaptations in Global Economies*, London: Sage Publishing Co.

Feldstein, M. S. (1974) 'Social Security, Induced Retirement, and Aggregate Capital Accumulation', *Journal of Political Economy*, vol. 85, no. 5.

Feldstein, M. S. & Horioka, C. (1980) 'Domestic Saving and International Capital Flows', *Economic Journal*, vol. 90, June.

Feldstein, M. S. & Siebert, H. eds. (2001) *Social Security Pension Reform in Europe*, Cambridge, MA.: NBER.

Fitoussi, J-P. & Le Cacheux, J. eds. (2002) *Rapport sur l'état de l'Union européenne 2002*, Paris: Fayard and Presses de Sciences Po.

Galeotti, G., Salmon, P. & Wintrobe, R. eds. (2000) *Competition and Structure, The Political Economy of Collective Decisions: Essays in Honor of Albert Breton*, Cambridge: Cambridge University Press.

INGENUE Team (2001) 'Macroeconomic Consequences of Pension Reforms in Europe: An Investigation with the INGENUE World Model', prepared for the Workshop *Ageing and International Capital Flows*, CPB, The Hague, 16-17 November, *OFCE Working Papers*, no. 2001-07, December ; also *CEPII Working Papers,* and *CEPREMAP Working Papers*.

INGENUE Team (2002) 'A Long-Term Model for the World Economy', in Hairault, J-O. & Kempf, H. (eds.) *Market Imperfections and Macroeconomic Dynamics*, Kluwer Academic Publishers.

Jousten, A. & Pestiau, P. (2000) 'Labor Mobility, Redistribution and Pension Reform in Europe', mimeograph, NBER Conference on Aging.

Le Cacheux, J. (2000) 'Labor Markets, Social Protection, Tax and Social Competition in the European Monetary Union', paper presented at the SALTSA Conference *Europe One Labor Market, Challenge for Workers and Employers*, Brussels, May 29-30, 2000; forthcoming in the conference volume.

Mc Morrow, K. & Roeger, W. (2002) 'EU Pension Reform – An Overview of the Debate and an Empirical Assessment of the Main Policy Reform Options', *European Commission Economic Papers*, no. 162.

Miles, D. & Timmermann, A. (1999) 'Risk Sharing and Transition Costs in the Reform of Pension Systems in Europe', *Economic Policy*, no. 29, October.

Observatoire des retraites, (2000) *L'Europe et la retraite*, Paris.

Reisen, H. (2000) *Pensions, Savings and Capital Flows*, OECD.

Salmon, P. (2000) 'Decentralization and Supranationality: The case of the European Union', paper presented at the Conference on *Fiscal Decentralization*, November 20-21, International Monetary Fund, Washington DC.

Sinn, H-W. (1997) 'The Selection Principle and Market Failure in Systems Competition', *Journal of Public Economics*, vol. 66, no. 2.

Sinn, H-W. (2001) 'European Integration and the Future of the Welfare State', *Swedish Economic Policy Review*, vol. 5.

Turner, D., Giorno, C., De Serres, A., Vourc'h, A. & Richardson, P. (1998) 'The Macroeconomic Implications of Aging in a Global Context', *OECD Economic Department Working Papers* no. 193.

Vernière, L. (2002) 'Panorama des réformes des systèmes de retraite à l'étranger : Etat des lieux et perspectives', *Questions Retraite*, Supplement, January.

Wildasin, D. E. (2000) 'Factor Mobility and Fiscal Policy in the EU: Policy Issues and Analytical Approaches', *Economic Policy*, October.